WHAT IS THE RELIGIOUS LIFE?
From the Gospels to Aquinas

WHAT IS THE RELIGIOUS LIFE?

From the Gospels to Aquinas

Aidan Nichols, O. P.

GRACEWING

First published in 2015

by

Gracewing
2 Southern Avenue
Leominster
Herefordshire
HR6 0QF

All rights reserved. No part of this publication may be reproduced, stored in a retrieval system, or transmitted in any form, or by any means, electronic, mechanical, photocopying, recording or otherwise, without the written permission of the publisher.

© 2015 Aidan Nichols, O.P.

The right of Aidan Nichols to be identified as the author of this work has been asserted in accordance with the Copyright, Designs and Patents Act, 1988.

ISBN 978 085244 886 1

Typesetting by
Action Publishing Technology Ltd, Gloucester GL1 5SR

Contents

Preface		*page* vii
1	Religious Life in the Apostolic Age	1
2	In the World of the Fathers: The Monks of Egypt	13
3	In the World of the Fathers: Palestine, Syria, Cappadocia	28
4	In the World of the Fathers: Latin Monasticism, and Notably St Augustine	42
5	From the Fathers, Especially St Benedict, to the Mediaevals	52
6	The Common Doctor: St Thomas Aquinas on the Religious Life	64
Conclusion		79
Index		83

Preface

My first experience of the Religious life was as a (rather short-lived) Benedictine postulant in the Yorkshire monastery of Ampleforth during the abbacy of Basil Hume, who later became Archbishop of Westminster and a greatly-loved public figure in England. The decision to go there, at the age of eighteen, and only as many months after my reception into the Catholic Church, was based on very limited knowledge. It turned largely on the fact that the son of my family's general practitioner was a monk of Ampleforth, though at the time on the 'mission' at one of the abbey's south Lancashire parishes. But though I did not persevere in the English Benedictine Congregation (my postulancy coincided with a very distracting dispute over my father's will), I still think my basic instinct had been correct. If you are going to become a Catholic, you might as well do it properly, assuming you are free so to do. In that case you will adopt the most radical – which is also the most simple and straightforward – life the Church affords. In other words, become (if male) a monk.

During my University years this aspiration altered in its character but did not change its focus. In becoming an English Dominican I hoped to amalgamate a monastic vocation with a doctrinal apostolate, and to do so in a more flexible situation than an abbey with an – at that time – labour-intensive boarding school to run as well as a raft of parishes to keep afloat. The crisis in the post-Conciliar Church which erupted in the later 1960s and '70s made this a more complicated procedure than I had expected. But the general tendency of the Dominicans since that time has been in the direction of the star I had glimpsed ahead. It is, after all, an Order whose founder was nourished on the *Conferences* of John Cassian, took as his guide the *Rule* of St Augustine, and was lauded by his successor in a *Libellus* or 'little book' that took as its model Athanasius' *Life of Anthony*, the charter of Egyptian monasticism. If these references mean little to the reader whose eye alights on this Preface, all will be revealed in due course. I could add to this chain of references that the Rule given by St Dominic to his second monastery of nuns, the enclosed contemplatives of San Sisto in Rome, has clear echoes of the Rule of St Benedict.

For the title of this short study, I have avoided the word 'monastic' which (in my experience) is somewhat neuralgic in the Order of Preachers in recent decades – though, I believe, unnecessarily so. Historically, it refers to the austerity of life expected of Dominicans, as seen notably in the 'regular observance' of which the four main concrete practices, still identified by the current Constitutions, are the wearing of the habit, enclosure, the use of silence, and 'penitential exercises'. (Examples of the latter would be fasting and keeping vigil by night-time meditation and prayer.) The phrase 'the Religious life' is the generally acceptable as well as the more comprehensive term for the radically simple discipleship typical of monks.

Where the word 'monastic' is virtually unavoidable, however, is when one wishes to draw attention to the classic sources of inspiration for the Religious life, which are found in the first eleven centuries of the Church's existence before Religious Orders had come to be, and above all in the patristic age, the epoch of the Fathers of the Church. What I describe in this book is the span of those centuries, though all the time keeping an eye on how the patristic (and early mediaeval) sources water the soil for the thirteenth-century flowering of the friars, the first major family of (if you will) 'post-monastic' Religious.

Appropriately, then, I close with St Thomas Aquinas, the great master of the thirteenth-century Schools. Not the least of the ways in which St Thomas Aquinas can be called the 'Common Doctor' of the Catholic Church lies in his synthetic doctrine of the Religious life, instructed by the monastic (i.e., pre-thirteenth century) sources of which he sees the life of the Order of Preachers as a creative variant and extension, and not a rejection or rupture. In my Conclusion I will say why I think that approach should be adopted in all theological reflection on 'consecrated' living in the Church.

Blackfriars, Cambridge
Memorial of Saints Basil and Gregory, 2015

1
Religious Life in the Apostolic Age

The idea of 'trajectory'

I begin from the New Testament and want to start by introducing the idea of a trajectory. The question is: Does Religious life, or, to use the older word, monasticism, have a basis in the New Testament? Catholic apologists have always argued, 'Yes!'. At the Reformation, the first Protestants, beginning with Luther, answered very definitely, 'No!'.[1] There is indeed hardly a simple answer to the question, but a helpful way in (I find) is provided by the idea of trajectories. 'Trajectory' is a term used in ballistics. It stands for the course executed by a missile when shot into the air. The trajectory idea was introduced into modern New Testament studies by two mid-twentieth-century scholars, Helmut Koester and James Robinson.[2] They argued that if you take your stand in the immediately post-apostolic period, rather than from within the period when the New Testament was written, certain trends or tendencies

---

[1] 'Judgement of Martin Luther on Monastic Vows', in H. Lehmann (ed.), *Luther's Works* 44 (Philadelphia, 1966), pp. 251–400. In fact Luther made an exception for Anthony of Egypt in whom, he held, faith far exceeded the role of monastic 'works and vows'. His fellow-Reformer Phillip Melanchthon would exclude from general censure both St Francis and St Dominic, for similar reasons.

[2] H. Koester and J. Robinson, *Trajectories through Early Christianity* (Philadelphia, 1971).

which you might otherwise have overlooked become plain. Koester and Robinson were not interested in defending classical Christian doctrine or practice. They were concerned with trying to work out the starting-point of the trajectory, not where it ended up. However their method lends itself to the purposes of more orthodox scholars. Thus, for instance, we can say that Unitarians, who deny the divinity of the Son and the Holy Spirit, and Trinitarian Christians, who affirm that divinity, disagree as to whether belief in the Holy Trinity is found in the pages of the New Testament, but as soon as you position yourself in the post-apostolic period it becomes plain that the New Testament has a Trinitarian 'trajectory'. Something similar can be said for monasticism or the Religious life. The evidence for it in the New Testament may be ambiguous but once you take your stand in the immediately post-apostolic period, you see that there is a trajectory starting up in the pages of the New Testament and pointing that way.

So far as Religious life is concerned, this turns out to be a *double* trajectory. One line of development involves the idea of Christian asceticism, a life of renunciation, where this world's goods, especially the prospect (or the actuality) of marriage and property, are surrendered for the sake of the Kingdom. That points to a form of dedicated virginity lived out in simplicity of life. The other trajectory begins from the practice of community of goods in a context of shared prayer and attention to the Word of God. That points to the idea of communitarian Religious life, the more technical term for which is 'coenobitic'.[3]

---

[3] For those who have the relevant languages, some useful discussions are: G. Kretschmar, 'Ein Beitrag zur Frage nach dem Ursprung frühchristliche Askese', *Zeitschrift für Theologie und Kirche* 61 (1964), pp. 27–67; T. Matura, *Célibat et communauté. Les fondements évangéliques de la Vie religieuse* (Paris, 1967); B. Lohse, *Askese und Mönchtum in der alten Kirche* (Munich, 1969); A. Guillaumont, *Aux origines du Monachisme chrétien. Pour une phénoménologie du monachisme* (Bellefontaine, 1979).

Jewish asceticism

In the case of monasticism (a word I'll use for the moment in preference to 'Religious life'), this approach can be complemented by another which suggests that – for the first and last time – monasticism was 'in the air' in Jewish life in the time just before and after the events described in the Gospels took place. If true, this claim creates a prejudice in favour of the trajectory mentioned. The Jewish asceticism in question was that of the 'Essenes' of Qumran. The Essenes were Jews who had separated themselves out from the rest of the people on the grounds that the Temple – at the time, the central institution of Judaism – had been defiled by the compromises of the high priesthood with Greek and, later, Roman paganism, whether in the persons of their rulers, in customs adopted, or in manners of thought entertained. The Essenes considered themselves to be the true Israel. The Qumran community was the most radical form Essenism took, because it was separate physically, as well as morally or mentally, being situated in the inhospitable landscape by the Dead Sea.[4] That is where the famous Dead Sea Scrolls were discovered in 1947. Quite what degree of influence Qumran had on primitive Christianity is open to question. John the Baptist is perhaps the most plausible candidate for a living link. Be that as it may, what is important for our subject is that, according to many, if not all, commentators, the Community Rule of Qumran portrays two groups: an inner circle and an outer.[5] The inner circle were celibates, and they practised community of goods. In the Community as a whole, a 'master' or 'guardian' was responsible for admitting candidates, teaching them the Rule, giving them spiritual instruction and looking after their pastoral welfare. The Qumran guardian might be compared to an

---

[4] See, for instance, J. Murphy-O'Connor, OP, 'The Essenes and their History', *Revue Biblique* 81 (1974), pp. 215–244.

[5] G. Vermes, 'The Community', in idem., *The Dead Sea Scrolls in English* (Harmondsworth, 1995, 4th edition, reprinted 1998), II, pp. 26–48.

abbot, especially if the latter were a layman, as many were, in a later Christian monastic group. Alongside the guardian was a priest who took responsibility for the community's worship, and notably for the common meal – apparently restricted to the inner circle of ascetics – where the messianic banquet was liturgically anticipated. The situation is remarkably reminiscent, at least verbally, of that in the Rule of St Augustine, where the two main officers mentioned are first, the *praepositus* or superior, originally in Augustine's communities a lay 'servant of God', i.e. a public celibate, and secondly, the *presbyter* or priest. Already in Augustine's lifetime St Jerome was pointing out the analogy between Christian monasticism and the Essene community inasmuch as the way of life of the latter had been briefly described by two Jewish writers, the historian Josephus and the philosopher Philo of Alexandria.[6]

Two New Testament motifs: i. virginity (and poverty)

In the New Testament itself, the first trajectory we need to consider is that of dedicated virginity lived in simplicity of life. When discussing with his disciples the topics of marriage and divorce, Jesus praises those who go so far as to make themselves 'eunuchs', celibates, for the sake of the Kingdom, the effective reign of God (Matthew 19:12).[7] Probably, this is praise of celibacy as a state more in harmony with the Kingdom of God than is marriage on the grounds that the voluntary 'eunuch' places himself at the service of God in a more thoroughgoing way. In Greek, 'Kingdom' is *basileia*, so I call this a 'basileological' rationale for the single life. It fits with this that in chapter 7 of St Paul's First Letter to the Corinthians, the apostle applauds the undivided loyalty in the Lord's service possible to the person who has not bound themselves

---

[6] Jerome, *Letters*, 22, to Eustochius.
[7] See Q. Quesnell, 'Made themselves eunuchs for the Kingdom of Heaven (Matthew 19:12)', *Catholic Biblical Quarterly* 30 (1968), pp. 336–359.

in marriage (cf. 1 Corinthians 7:34). The community, he implies, needs some people who will live exclusively for its specific ends. This is the biblical text Pope John Paul II chose to put first in *Vita consecrata*, his post-synodal apostolic exhortation on 'the consecrated life and its mission in the Church and the world', in 1996.[8] These are the people, presumably, whom St John has in mind in the Book of the Apocalypse, when he describes the heavenly honour given to virgins who, he says, 'follow the Lamb wherever he goes' (14:4). In time, a distinction will be drawn between continence, as practised by the secular clergy in the West – a higher pragmatism, the rationale of which is the more exclusive availability to the faithful that it makes possible on the part of priests – and religious chastity, or what St Thomas will call *pia virginitas*, the point of which he says is 'to be vacant, *vacare*, more freely for divine contemplation'.[9]

When we turn to the post-apostolic end of the trajectory, 'virgins', female and male, are evidently a distinct group in the Church. Thus at the end of the first Christian century we find Ignatius of Antioch greeting 'the virgins' (female) in the Church at Smyrna,[10] and in his letter to Polycarp, Ignatius warns virgins (this time male virgins are in mind) not to claim moral superiority for themselves when compared with other disciples.

> If anyone can remain in continence to the honour of the flesh of the Lord, let him do so without boasting.[11]

Almost exactly the same words are used at about the same time by Pope St Clement writing to the Church in Corinth.[12] In the second century, the Apologist Athenagoras reports that there were in the Church what he calls 'many men and women

---

[8] John Paul II, *Vita Consecrata*, 1.
[9] Thomas Aquinas, *Summa theologiae* IIa. IIae., q. 152, a. 7.
[10] Ignatius, *To the Smyrniots*, XIII.1.
[11] Idem., *To Polycarp*, V.2.
[12] Clement of Rome, *First Letter to the Corinthians* 38, 2.

who have grown old without marrying in the hope of being of service to God'.[13]

Such scattered allusions furnish only hints about the motivation of these *virgines* or *continentes*. But with regard to the origin of the trajectory – the Saviour's praise of those who have become eunuchs for the sake of the Kingdom – we are on safe ground in saying Jesus regarded celibacy as a sign of the messianic age when God was to be all in all. To be able to live exclusively for God, seeking no human partner, offering all one's powers, including sexual powers, as a joyful sacrifice, this is a sign of the last age of the world when the covenant relationship of God and humanity is taking on a previously unknown intimacy or closeness.

Then at the end of the trajectory, there's a huge patristic literature on the life of virgins, starting with texts from the early ecclesiastical writers before the Council of Nicaea (325). These span the whole range from North Africa (Tertullian and Cyprian) to Asia Minor (Methodius of Olympus) and Egypt (Clement of Alexandria). We can take Methodius as fairly typical. For Methodius, by his or her complete dedication to the mystery of salvation the virgin constitutes the perfect actualisation of the Church. Moreover, she or he is, as he puts it, betrothed to the Word. Accordingly, in Methodius's dialogue *The Banquet*, which is modelled on Plato's *Symposium* (both are, in effect, discussions of the nature and consequences of love), we are given for the understanding of what a virgin is an ecclesiological theme ('perfect actualisation of the Church') and a mystical theme ('betrothed to the Word').[14]

In *Vita consecrata*, John Paul II joins these two themes together when he writes that the consecrated life manifests

---

[13] Athenagoras, *Supplication for the Christians*, 33.
[14] Methodius, *Convivium* II. 1, VII. 2. I follow the interpretation of J. Daniélou in *History of Early Christian Doctrine II. The Gospel and Hellenistic Culture* (London, 1963), pp. 292–293.

'the striving of the whole Church as Bride towards union with her one Spouse', though the pope adds a coda to the effect that this should encourage the Christian people at large to greater fidelity: an encouraging idea that goes beyond anything Methodius says explicitly.[15]

Then in the two centuries after Nicaea, in the patristic golden age, we have treatises on the subject of virginity from Eastern Fathers like Athanasius, John Chrysostom, Gregory of Nyssa, and Western ones such as Jerome, Ambrose and Augustine. The Dominican patrologist Thomas Camelot went so far as to say that, aside from treatises on martyrdom and commentaries on the Lord's Prayer and not forgetting, as he puts it, 'the rich treasures of spiritual doctrine scattered through the homilies of Origen', there are not before the end of the fourth century any other 'spiritual' writings than those on virginity.[16]

Very likely, it is significant that so many of the authors of these treatises were bishops. Gradually, the virgins were ceasing to practise a domestic asceticism, whereby in the immediately sub-apostolic period they had lived in the family home but avoiding luxuries and worldly entertainments and devoted themselves to prayer and works of charity (not that domestic asceticism died out – Catherine of Siena and Rose of Lima are examples in the fourteenth and sixteenth centuries respectively), and instead were becoming semi-institutionalised groups under the special care of the local bishop. We can hear a bishop seeking actively to affect the life of virgins when in his treatise *On Virginity* Athanasius urges virgins to adopt a rule of life with fixed hours of prayer, habitual fasting until the ninth hour and the meditative reading of Scripture.[17] Such a development would foreshadow the later utilisation of

---

[15] John Paul II, *Vita consecrata*, 3.
[16] T. Camelot, OP, *Virgines Christi, La Virginité aux premiers siècles de l'Eglise* (Paris, 1944), p. 48.
[17] Athanasius, *De virginitate*, 16.

Religious life by bishops (and subsequently popes) who saw it as an exceptionally valuable resource, which could well be put to various uses in the wider Church.

Many bishops were, in any case, monk-bishops. Hagiographical sources tend to accord such bishops higher spiritual authority.[18] And one thing such bishops tended to do was to attempt to monasticise their own clergy. So when in the introduction to his *Life of Anthony* Athanasius more or less dedicates the *Life* to what he calls 'monks in foreign parts' who are seeking to emulate Anthony's example, he may be thinking not only of those leading a hermit life in the West but of Western bishops like Hilary of Poitiers who encouraged their clergy to adopt a monastic form of living.[19]

I said that such virginity was lived out in 'simplicity of life'. The topic of the renunciation of goods surfaces in the words Jesus addresses to the Rich Young Man a little later in chapter 19 of St Matthew's Gospel (verses 16-22). Jesus calls the rich young man to sell all that he has in order to follow him, the one who is the Bearer of the Kingdom.[20] Again, as with virginity itself, the thinking seems to be that the renunciation of worldly goods fits better with the life of the Kingdom. The rich are weighed down by the goods of this world. So, although there is a place for them in the Kingdom, it takes all the force of God's grace to propel them through the gate of the poor. Possessions are, basileologically speaking, a distraction, as modern consumerism underlines.

At the other, post-apostolic, end of the trajectory, it's significant that the most common word for ascetics in Egyptian Christian sources is 'renouncers', *apotaktikoi*, people who practised 'renunciation', *apotagê* – meaning, presumably, first

---

[18] P. Rousseau, 'The Spiritual Authority of the Monk-Bishop. Eastern Elements in some Western Hagiography of the Fourth and Fifth Centuries', *Journal of Theological Studies*, 22 (1971), pp. 380–419.

[19] J. Herrin, *The Formation of Christendom* (Oxford, 1987), p. 66.

[20] J. Legasse, *L'Appel du riche (Marc 10:17–31 et par.): Contribution à l'étude des fondements scripturaires de la Vie religieuse* (Paris, 1966).

and foremost, renunciation of property, of material goods. In the fourth century, St Ambrose, according to the biography of him by one of his presbyters, Paulinus, gave away all his property on becoming a bishop so that he might be able to 'follow Christ the Lord'.[21]

As a bishop of this period with not only ecclesiastical but also civil duties, Ambrose could be regarded as living only a *quasi*-monastic existence. So a much clearer example comes with the *Life of Anthony* by St Athanasius. As well as recording the memory of an historic personality, the *Life of Anthony* is a book that commends the monastic life to the wider Church. In it we find that Anthony discovered his ascetic vocation when he heard read out in church the gospel of the Rich Young Man. He had just walked to church through his village:

> considering [writes Athanasius] how the apostles, forsaking everything, followed the Saviour [cf. Matthew 4:20], and how in Acts some sold what they possessed and took the proceeds and placed them at the feet of the apostles for distribution among those in need [Acts 4:35].[22]

So here it's the summons to evangelical poverty that triggers the call to radical asceticism. In parenthesis we can note that a call to be with Jesus by renouncing both property and family ties echoes Jesus' own original call to his first disciples, a call which is earlier than their appointment to the apostolic ministry. Using later terminology: the apostles were first of all Religious and only then priests.

The rationale for a life of renunciation of marriage and goods in the New Testament can be called not only 'basileological', Kingdom-oriented, but also 'soteriological', meaning to do with salvation, in that such renunciation is evidently concerned with optimising the conditions for our appropriation of salvation in Jesus Christ.

---

[21] Paulinus, *Life of Ambrose*, 38.
[22] Athanasius, *Life of Anthony*, 2.

These two renunciations – of property and of marriage and family – form the heart of what were later called the evangelical counsels of poverty and chastity and, I would argue, that of obedience also. 'Obedience', considered as a feature of future Christian monasticism, has its basis in the Gospels inasmuch as it consists in the willingness to heed and follow through the call of the Lord to poverty and chastity.[23]

Two New Testament motifs: ii. common life

Athanasius's reference in the *Life of Anthony* to the way of life of the apostolic Church in the Acts of the Apostles brings me (if more briefly) to the second of the New Testament trajectories, that of the common life. The Jerusalem Church had at its core a group of believers sharing a community life which was marked by attendance at the celebration of the Eucharist and at what St Luke calls 'the prayers': acts of worship modelled, in all probability, on the Jewish prayer hours. For obvious reasons, as long as the Church was subject to periodic persecution, it was difficult for this kind of public common life to have imitators. But soon after the Peace of the Church, in the early fourth century, coenobitic life emerges simultaneously in widely separated regions such as Egypt and Cappadocia (now east-central Turkey).

By the fifth century, the life of such communities begins to be described as an 'apostolic' life, meaning the kind of corporate life lived by the apostles at Jerusalem immediately after the Ascension. Behind that, in the pre-Ascension period, we could, if we wished, see the life Jesus' friends shared with their Master during his public ministry, a common life which also had an atmosphere of prayer (summed up in the giving of the Our Father), and a common purse (held by Judas Iscariot).

---

[23] On the counsels in the Gospels generally, see, in addition to the titles given in note 3 above, F. Mussner, 'Die evangelische Räte und das Evangelium', *Benediktine Monatschrift* 30 (1954), pp. 485–493.

Proto-eucharistically, that life of the disciples with their Master took Jesus himself, the Bread of Life, as its central focus. So there is a similarity of structure between the life of the disciples during the public ministry, their life at the time of Pentecost and its immediate aftermath, and the life of coenobites in the later Church. Writing in the middle decades of the thirteenth century, Thomas Aquinas will say of the Jerusalem Church portrayed in Acts 4, 'It is from that holy community that the [common] life took its birth, as is related in *The Conferences of the Fathers*',[24] the synopsis of the wisdom of the early Egyptian monks produced by a late fourth-century Latin visitor, John Cassian (on whom more anon).

In describing the coenobitic way as 'apostolic', we have an implicitly ecclesiological rationale for the Religious life, as a communion centred on listening to the Word in a liturgically framed existence with the Eucharist as its centre. That makes a coenobitic group an icon of the Church as a whole. But the monastic church has two distinctive features not shared by the wider Church as such: it is a communion where fraternity includes having all things in common: i.e. its members practise poverty conceived here not so much as the individual renunciation of goods but rather as their corporate possession, and its life is that of celibates without spouse or children.

Despite the importance of this concept of the monastic micro-church, when we look back on the trajectories we have followed, it seems to me that dedicated virginity is actually the fundamental impulse in Christian monasticism. The common life of Christian Religious is essentially a life lived by virgins who enter into fellowship with each other. But that common life dimension is not simply a convenient add-on, based in practical considerations about how to fund oneself. It has, after all, a genuine Gospel trajectory of its own. The coming together of the two trajectories (virginity, with simplicity, and

---

[24] Thomas Aquinas, *On the First Letter of St Paul to the Corinthians*, XVI, lect. 1, where Thomas is citing Cassian's *Conferences*, XVIII.4.

the common life) is a very happy convergence. A community of virgins, as distinct from a set of virgins living apart, whether as domestic ascetics or as what a later generation would call 'hermits', gives expression to the Church as a communion in the service of the Kingdom, that Kingdom where one lives one hundred per cent for God, a life to which dedicated virginity, especially when combined with the renunciation of goods, eloquently gestures and does so at the request of the Incarnate Word himself.

2

In the World of the Fathers: The Monks of Egypt

I turn now to the patristic age, the age of the Fathers, not so much (as hitherto) because it provides a window on what the New Testament authors may have been getting at (the 'trajectory' concept) but for its own sake. My aim here is to show how the two motifs of consecrated virginity and the common life developed in the age of the Fathers, while also asking how the monastics of these centuries expressed theologically the various dimensions of their calling – whether they saw it as soteriological (concerned with salvation), Christological (as some sort of imitation of the life of Christ), ecclesiological (an expression of the mystery of the Church), or whatever. Our first port of call is Egypt.

St Anthony the Great

St Anthony, born in 251, is called the 'father of monks',[1] but we know he was not the very first. Quite apart from the early ascetics, the *virgines, continentes* and *apotaktikoi* we looked at in the last chapter – the 'proto-monastics' living chiefly in domestic settings – we find prior to Anthony a hermit, described for us by St Jerome, in the Nile Valley.[2] This was St Paul of Thebes,

---

[1] N. Devilliers, *Saint Antoine le Grand, père des moines* (Bellefontaine, 1971).
[2] Jerome, *Life of Paul*. An English translation is provided by Helen Waddell in her anthology *The Desert Fathers* (London, 1962 [1936]), pp. 37–62.

later popular among the illiterate hermits who, in mediaeval England, supported themselves by acting as repairers of bridges and highways.[3] In another example, a bishop from Upper Egypt present at the Council of Nicaea was said to have lived in an *askêtikon*, an ascetic's cell, for 'many years'.[4]

One clue as to the possible origin of figures like this comes from an early fourth-century Alexandrian source from which we hear that around 250, during the persecution of the Church by the emperor Decius, which is believed to have been particularly severe in Egypt, many Christians fled to the desert and mountains and lived there in solitude.[5] Possibly some of them never came back. At any rate, when Jerome wrote his short life of Paul of Thebes this is the explanation he offers for how it was Paul came to take up the eremitical life.

An alternative explanation is given in the first Greek life of St Pachomius, a younger contemporary of Anthony. Early monks wanted to emulate the maximalism of the martyrs of the previous generation, their complete self-giving, and asceticism was the way they found to do it.[6]

The *Life of Anthony* itself mentions both women ascetics, into whose care the young Anthony placed his sister, and also, in the neighbourhood of Anthony's village, an elderly man who had given himself to a life of asceticism from boyhood. Whether these people were in any sense products of the persecution we have no idea, but Anthony spent the first phase of his monastic life studying their practices and virtues.

What emerges from the wider picture, then, is not that Anthony was in any obvious sense a new start. It's more that in

---

[3] V. Davis, 'The Rule of St Paul, the First Hermit, in Medieval England', in W. J. Shiels (ed.), *Monks, Hermits and the Ascetic Tradition* (Oxford, 1985), pp. 203–214.
[4] See E. R. Hardy, *Christian Egypt. Church and People* (Oxford, 1952), p. 39.
[5] The witness is Dionysius of Alexandria; for a parallel claim in the Cappadocian context, see L. Bouyer, 'The Origins of Monasticism', in *idem.*, *The Spirituality of the New Testament and the Fathers* (London, 1963), p. 305.
[6] The First Greek Life of Pachomius, 1.

Anthony the ascetic movement became conscious of its own significance in the life of the Church and found a leader capable of drawing numbers of people to itself. By writing Anthony's life, Athanasius was commending that movement to the episcopate. Increasingly, bishops would not only make use of ascetics but be drawn from their ranks as well.[7]

We can look more closely at what Anthony was doing. By a radical 'withdrawal', *anachôrêsis* (hence our word 'anchorite'), Anthony – whose dates are usually given as c. 251 to 356 – began to live somewhere on the boundary between the cultivated arable land and the desert, where he found some abandoned tombs, a legacy of the old Egyptian paganism. He used the tombs – presumably this means their masonry – so as to create a dwelling. Because Christian Copts regarded the ancient Pharaonic paganism as quasi-demonic, shadowed by the influence of the fallen angels, the view is plausible that this choice of accommodation was symbolic. Anthony was acting out exposure to demons, and notably to inner 'demons': that is, to the influence on his heart and mind of his own disordered thoughts and feelings. Holy warfare with elements in one's own psyche that are alien to charity will be, in the future, a major theme of the desert fathers.

Subsequently, Anthony moved away from the boundaries of the desert into an area of true desert. This was situated to the east of the Nile where he found a convenient cave at a place called Pispir. There he became the leader of a colony of hermits. Finally, when he was about sixty years old, his thirst for solitude drove him to a remoter spot, the so-called 'Mountain of St Anthony' near the Red Sea coast. Even so, monks still came to him for counsel and his sayings began to be widely known.

---

[7] P. Rousseau, *Ascetics, Authority and the Church in the Age of Jerome and Cassian* (Oxford, 1978). That did not prevent some bishops experiencing monks as rivals for spiritual leadership, and seeking more to control them than to utilize them (much less emulate them). See R. Finn, OP, *Asceticism in Greco-Roman Antiquity* (Cambridge, 2009), pp. 149–155.

The themes Athanasius associates with Anthony are much the same as those ascribed to him in the short comments which were passed down under his name in the collection called 'The Sayings of the Fathers'. The text called the *Apophthegmata Patrum* (an 'apophthegm' is a pithy saying) belongs to the sixth century but scholars think that the sayings it contains may have begun to circulate in oral form as early as the fourth century, and thus possibly in Anthony's own lifetime. In both the *Life of Anthony* and the Sayings tradition, the goal of renunciation (we have already encountered that concept and the Greek word that stands for it, *apotagê*) could be described as *freedom from anxiety*, the point of which is to enable the person to enjoy the presence of God and live in innocence, as in a new paradise. This entails further aspects: physical asceticism, notably by abstinence from food; a continual awareness of the reality of divine judgment; compunction for sin; struggle with the demons, i.e. our harmful thoughts and temptations and, finally, the 'discernment of spirits', meaning the assessment of the positive or negative value for sanctification of one's emotions and states of mind.

The importance of this material for Christian spirituality is presumably obvious: these are all features that need factoring into any account of growth in holiness, or what came to be called 'the theology of Christian perfection'.

Some critics feel there is little that is clearly evangelical in all this. But in the seven extant letters of Anthony, now once again regarded as genuine, Anthony identifies the ultimate basis of the ascetic way in terms of the Christian economy of salvation.[8] Its foundation is the infinite love of the God who, in salvation history, deigned time and again to 'visit' his human creatures. This was already happening in the patriarchs and prophets but above all it took place in the Incarnation. These gracious interventions of God in human history– his Covenants – place upon

---

[8] S. Rubenson, *The Letters of St Antony. Monasticism and the Making of a Saint* (Minneapolis, 1995).

us the obligation to respond appropriately, by using all human powers in the pursuit of perfect holiness.[9] Otherwise the coming of the Saviour will be for us a cause of condemnation, rather than the opposite.

It is speculated that Athanasius intended his *Life of Anthony* to be a Christian counterpart to the *Life of Plotinus*, the pagan philosopher and mystic, written by Plotinus's gifted disciple and philosophical successor, Porphyry. There are obvious differences between the two figures, since one was a literate but otherwise uneducated Christian peasant and the other was an intellectually sophisticated pagan urbanite, the founder of the Neo-Platonist school. Interest in comparing the two men – and the two *Lives* – turns mainly on the difference in their views of holiness, and especially on what these texts have to say or imply about the usefulness or otherwise of traditional education and culture – lumped together by the Greeks in the term *paideia* – as a way to attain it. For Porphyry, so one student of early monasticism writes:

> Conversion to philosophy meant a profound inward reorientation in which one was in a sense reborn into a new awareness of everything most sublime in the cultural tradition.[10]

Likewise, St Anthony represented a conversion, reorientation, and new birth. But the 'culture' (*paideia*) recommended by Anthony and the other desert fathers was, in the words of the same modern writer:

> a new *paideia*, born of the silence and solitude of the desert and of the Word of God.[11]

---

[9] Anthony, *Letters*, 3.
[10] D. Burton-Christie, *The Word in the Desert. The Quest for Holiness in Early Christian Monasticism* (New York, 1993), p. 49. See also J.-C. Guy, 'Educational Innovation in the Desert Fathers', *Eastern Churches Review* 6 (1974), pp. 44–51
[11] D. Burton-Christie, *The Word in the Desert*, op. cit., p. 54. See further, A. Louth, 'St Athanasius and the Greek Life of Anthony', *Journal of Theological Studies*, n. s. 39 (1988), pp. 504–509; G. Gould, 'The *Life of Anthony* and the

It's a culture of *lectio divina*, of biblical spirituality, and insofar as it has, in later monastics, a love of learning, this love is governed and penetrated by a desire for the personal God.

Mention of the 'desert fathers' in the plural reminds us that the monastic 'culture', if that be the right word to use, was not for a handful of fervent devotees. It was popular enough to be demographically significant. The monastic population of Egypt before the seventh-century Arab invasion is thought to have been numbered in thousands. Partly for this reason, one study of early Christian monasticism is entitled 'The Desert a City'.[12]

I have one further comment to report before leaving the Antonian moment behind. It has been suggested that by calling the desert monks the desert *fathers*, patristic age Christians were drawing a comparison between the monks and the theologians, many of them bishops, whom we refer to as 'the Fathers of the Church'. Both groups had things to teach, the monks from silence and solitude, the bishop-theologians from study, argument, and the transmission of the magisterial tradition in the apostolic succession.[13]

Semi-eremitical and eremitical life

Most of the desert fathers lived in Lower Egypt, between what is now Cairo and Alexandria. One important grouping occupied the edge of a large lake, partly water, partly swampy

---

Origins of Christian Monasticism in Fourth Century Egypt', *Medieval History* 1 (1991), pp. 3–11. A classic monograph is L. Bouyer, *La vie de saint Antoine. Essai sur la spiritualité du monachisme primitive* (Bellefontaine, 1977). For how the Latin Middle Ages saw him, and this is pertinent to Blessed Jordan of Saxony's portrayal of St Dominic (cf. my Preface), see J. Leclerq, 'S. Antoine dans la tradition monastique médiévale', *Studia Anselmiana* 38 (1956), pp. 229–247.

[12] D. Chitty, *The Desert a City. An Introduction to the Study of Egyptian and Palestinian Monasticism under the Christian Empire* (Oxford, 1966).

[13] B. Ward, 'Introduction', *The Desert Fathers. Sayings of the Early Christian Monks* (London, 2003), pp. ix–x.

ground, which joined Alexandria to its southern hinterland. This was the monastic colony of Nitria, some miles south-east of the city. It was partly eremitical, partly coenobitic: a model which would later be repeated in Palestine, where it was given the Greek name *laura* meaning a pathway (a route connecting hermitages is the general idea). This word entered Russian as *lavra* and from Greek or Russian has reached the Western languages in the modern period. Considered as a lavra, Nitria resembled a village of scattered houses with, at its centre, some important shared buildings. These consisted of a refectory for common meals and a church where the monks would gather for the evening and night offices on Saturdays and Sundays – the vigil of Sunday being an extended celebration which ended with Lauds and the Eucharistic Liturgy.

Nitria has been called the gateway to the desert, rather than the desert itself.[14] Further south and west lay real desert, the desert of Scetis, while in between lay some settlements known as *Kellia*, 'The Cells'. These represented a halfway house, metaphorically as well as literally, between Nitria and Scetis. Here the monks' dwellings were so far removed from each other as to be out of earshot one from another, though their occupants seem to have depended on Nitria to get their basic foodstuffs.

We know from the sources that the inhabitants of *Kellia* would sometimes gather in groups for recitation of the Scriptures, with a special focus on the Psalms, though such spiritual exercises could also be carried out by each monk alone.

Contrastingly, the monks of Scetis, the true desert, considered themselves called to a life of perpetual solitude, broken only by occasional visits from those who sought their counsel

---

[14] The correct topography for these places was first established for twentieth-century students by Evelyn White in his ground-breaking – literally! – book *History of the Monasteries of Nitria and of Scetis* (London, 1932), though actual excavation did not begin until 1965. The real Nitria had disappeared off the map, and had become confused with the modern Wadi-el-Natrun, which is actually Scetis, the true desert.

or by exceptional calls on their charity. Typically, they treated their cells as what have been called workshops of prayer, and this was not least a prayer of militant intercession on behalf of Christendom, as in the saying attributed to Abba Macarius of Alexandria: 'I am guarding the walls'.

This saying is interesting not least because it is an example of someone working out a statement of the *ecclesiological* value of monasticism. Macarius was seeking to establish his role (and by implication that of other monastics) in the wider communion of the Church, as distinct from treating his calling as of purely personal significance: important only for the spiritual life of this or that individual wanting to grow in stature as a disciple of Christ. No doubt it is from the more reflective monks like Macarius that the great majority of the sayings of the desert fathers have come down to us.

Those sayings are arranged in two sorts of collections. One type is alphabetical (i. e. laid out according to the names of the monks, in alphabetical order).[15] The other is systematic (i.e. laid out according to themes).[16] In either form, these collections of sayings carry on the sort of reflection that Anthony started. Most of their content could be described by the phrase 'existential wisdom', wisdom for existence, for everyday living. In the Orthodox Church of Greece, these books are called today the *Gerontikon* or 'Book of the Elders', or alternatively, the *Paterikon* or 'Book of the Fathers', and they are very widely used as sourcebooks not only for ascetic teaching but also for moral theology. This is not so surprising because to quote again the twentieth-century author who wrote about ancient monasticism as an alternative culture:

---

[15] Benedicta Ward, *The Sayings of the Desert Fathers. The Alphabetical Collection* (London, 1975).

[16] J. Dion – G. Oury, *Les sentences des Pères du désert* (Solesmes, 1966–1981, 4 volumes) is comprehensive for both types.

IN THE WORLD OF THE FATHERS: THE MONKS OF EGYPT

> The silence and solitude of the desert ... which so clearly revealed the hidden motivations of the heart, focussed the attention of the desert fathers upon moral, ascetical and psychological questions in a particularly acute way.[17]

St John Cassian

This was the tradition summed up by St John Cassian whose series of extended interviews with the Egyptian fathers, titled by him 'The Conferences', would have a tremendous impact in the West on the spirituality of monastics and other Religious (they were, for example, in the late twelfth century the favourite spiritual reading of the founder of the Order of Preachers, St Dominic).

John Cassian was a Westerner, or at any rate a native Latin-speaker (his family may have lived in what is now Romania). Born around 360, and the recipient of a good classical education, he travelled first to Palestine and then to Egypt in search of monastic wisdom, prior to entering a community of monks in Bethlehem about the year 390. Gaining permission to visit the monasteries of Egypt, what was described as a short tour of inspection was somehow prolonged into a stay of several years. Pardoned by his community for this unscripted absence, he was permitted to go off on his travels a second time: someone realized the potential importance of what he was doing. These journeys were in fact serious-minded investigations of the Egyptian monastic settlements of the day, made with a monk companion who later became a bishop. While in Nitria, Cassian became embroiled in the bitter controversy which had broken out over the orthodoxy of the

---

[17] D. Burton-Christie, *The Word in the Desert*, op. cit., p. 61. This author speaks of an entire 'desert hermeneutic' for reading Scripture. In effect, this is what some Church Fathers and mediaeval authors call the 'tropological' sense of the biblical text.

Alexandrian exegete and theologian Origen.[18] Fleeing to Constantinople, he was ordained deacon by St John Chrysostom. Some time around 410, having received the priesthood, probably in Rome, he settled finally in Provence where his career as a writer began.

In Cassian's day, pure eremitism, the life of Scetis, and even semi-eremitism, the life of Nitria and the Cells, were giving way in Egypt to a more organized coenobitic style of living. Cassian felt ambivalent about this development. At one level, he thought, it was sensible, since it would discourage monastic idiosyncracy. But at another level, it threatened the survival of the desert spirit. This ambivalence explains the structure of the literature he left behind for use in the Latin West.

His book *The Institutes* is devoted to the organisation of monasteries, including the structure of the liturgical day, as well as with guidance for monks on how to correct basic faults. Cassian thought of this first book as helpful for training what he termed the 'outer man'. In other words, he hoped it would turn out to be a useful guide for helping monks to develop a self-discipline that would enable harmonious co-existence with others, cultivating relevant virtues and discouraging equally relevant vices.

His other work, *The Conferences*, which was much the more influential of the two, was ostensibly written for anchorites. But it is better understood as mainly concerned with the 'inner man': in other words, it was intended for coenobites who were striving after the sort of spiritual perfection which the monastic tradition associated above all with the desert, with Scetis. As the Cassian scholar Columba Stewart has put it:

---

[18] For the impact of this controversy on desert monasticism see D. Chitty, *The Desert a City*, op. cit., pp. 58–59. The conflict set at odds a section of the monastic population who seem to have had a naively anthropomorphic view of God and such highly educated monks as the 'Tall Brothers' who eventually left Nitria, with some three hundred others, for Jerusalem, Scythopolis (in Palestine) and Constantinople.

In the original plan of his monastic writings, Scetis typified the culmination of monastic progress. The *Institutes* were to present coenobitic rules; the *Conferences*, attributed to monks of Scetis, were to emphasize the contemplative dedication that surpassed the disciplinary focus of coenobitic life.[19]

As things turned out, then, Cassian's distinction between coenobitic and anchoritic (or eremitic) operates less as a way of discriminating between two kinds of monastic life and more as a way of describing the progress of each and any monk towards the goal of monastic living in general. Monastic progress means moving through the 'practical' life of developing the virtues to the 'contemplative' life where, through purity of heart, the monk has a foretaste of the vision of God.

The monasteries Cassian envisaged for the West had far more by way of liturgical life than would have been possible in Nitria, let alone The Cells or Scetis. The liturgical day Cassian proposes (and here he was setting a model for later monastic founders) is structured by six 'hours' or Offices. Two of these – the evening Office, Vespers, and the night Office, Matins combined with Lauds – were derived from Egyptian use. Three, the day hours of Terce, Sext and None, formed, as he knew, a normal part of monastic practice in the monasteries of Greater Syria, of which Palestine was part. The morning Office of Prime, said before work began, came from his own Palestinian experience in his home monastery in Bethlehem. Such Offices, he says, are a good thing, because set times of prayer help weak human beings to praise God. But better still would be for monks to pray and make psalmody quasi-unceasingly, as happened in the desert.

This could be described as a rather 'low' doctrine of the divine Office, for it presents 'official' prayer, the Prayer of the Hours, as something that is distinctly second best. Here Cassian would not be followed by St Benedict, who otherwise learned a lot from him. Benedict was influenced, rather, by the

---

[19] C. Stewart, *Cassian the Monk* (New York, 1998), p. 10.

experience of ascetics who gathered round the Roman basilicas, which were major centres of liturgical life. Nor did the Augustinian tradition (vital for the later Orders of canons regular and their offshoots) accept that liturgical prayer in community should be counted a poor second. That tradition, at least from the time of Augustine's second monastery, at Hippo Regius, had been formulated in explicit association with the church and house of the bishop, who is the chief liturgist of the local church.

In other respects, however, by which I mean in regard to his theology of monasticism and indeed his spiritual doctrine in general, Cassian was, as already intimated, enormously influential in later centuries, at any rate until the end of the Middle Ages, so much so that one historian can say that every subsequent school of Christian spirituality has had recourse, knowingly or not, to Cassian's ascetic principles.[20]

Pachomius

The last Egyptian figure we should look at is St Pachomius, who is chronologically the first known coenobitic founder.

In the valley of the Upper Nile, defined as lying between Cairo, to the north, and Luxor and the first Cataract to the south, there grew up, at the same time as the semi-eremitic and eremitic movement down river, a fully coenobitic monasticism centred on the figure of St Pachomius.[21] Pachomius was born around 290 to pagan parents and became a Christian through contacts made when a conscript in the imperial army. At first he lived a life modeled on the hermits but around 320 he moved to Tabennesi, a deserted village near the Nile, and established there a community under the authority of a

---

[20] M. Augé, 'Tra l'Oriente e l'Occidente: Evagrio Pontico e Giovanni Cassiano', in idem., E. Sastre Santos, L. Borriello, *Storia della vita religiosa* (Brescia, 1988), p. 80.

[21] P. Rousseau, *Pachomius. The Making of a Community in Fourth Century Egypt* (Berkeley, CA, 1985).

neighbouring bishop. He was to be the first superior in a strictly communitarian type of monasticism. Pachomius expected his monks to cultivate the nearby agricultural land and also to make the effort to become literate, so as to be able to read the Scriptures and celebrate the Liturgy, which last was accorded great importance.[22] The combination of manual labour, Scripture reading and an intense liturgical life was to become classic for coenobitic monasticism, especially in the West. Pachomius was, in effect, an amalgam of administrator and spiritual leader, rather like the 'guardian' at Qumran. The Pachomian Rule is the first coenobitic Rule in Christian history, and the need it created for abbots somehow to juggle the two roles, spiritual father and administrator would remain a challenge that cenobites elsewhere also had to face.

Pachomian Religious life took the form of alternative village societies made up of hundreds of largely peasant monks. Ten monasteries were founded by Pachomius himself, including one for women. The dominant spiritual motif was mutual service. Thus, for example, in his fifth letter, Pachomius writes:

> We work, bearing one another's burdens as Christ took our infirmities on his own body and did not spare himself.[23]

Previously, up until about the year 320, when he was in his early 30s, Pachomius had lived a solitary life on the Antonian model. But while keeping solitary vigil in prayer, asking to be taught the perfect will of God, he had a vision of an angel who said, 'The will of God is to minister to the human race, to reconcile men to him'.[24] Basing himself on this inspiration, Pachomius proceeded to found a monastery at a place called

---

[22] A. Veilleux, OCR, *La Liturgie dans le cénobitisme pachômien au quatrième siècle* (Rome, 1968).

[23] A. Boon (ed.), *Pachomiana latina. Règle et Epîtres de s. Pachôme. Epître de s. Théodore et 'Liber' de s. Orsiesius* (Louvain, 1932), p. 92. Characteristically, this short statement is a fusion of two biblical allusions (Galatians 6:1 and Matthew 8:17).

[24] First Greek Life of Pachomius, 23.

Tabennisis where he sought to realise his vision by putting his organizational skills at the service of other monks and, in his exposition of monastic doctrine, encouraging them to serve one another in daily living.[25]

Here, then, is a second sort of what I called an 'ecclesiological' explanation for the Religious life in the Egyptian setting. This is not, as it was with Macarius in Lower Egypt, a matter of militant intercession on behalf of the Christian city. Here in Upper Egypt we encounter instead the concept of a monastery as a model of redeemed community. The coenobium expresses the communion of the Church in the Church's task of uniting people with each other and with God. A Pachomian monastery was intended as a community of reconciliation, where men are helped to find God by each other and especially by the abbot, whose teaching role in catechetical explanation of the Scriptures is emphasised in the first Greek *Life* of this saint.

In the writings of subsequent generations of Pachomian abbots much is made (not surprisingly) of the example of the apostolic community in Jerusalem where all had one heart and one soul. Later, in the West, this becomes – once more, highly influentially – the starting-point of the Rule of Augustine.

The Pachomian Rule anticipates Augustine and Benedict in its concern for the weaker brethren. Yet at the same time it maintains a high ideal of monastic and notably liturgical observance. Thus the night Office was to last from midnight until dawn, estimated as being in southern Egypt about, on average, four hours.

What is possibly our first evidence for the wearing of a distinctive monastic habit comes from the Pachomian sources.[26] Thanks to a Latin translation, by St Jerome, of the

---

[25] Ibid., 25.
[26] P. Oppenheim, *Das Mönchskleid im christlichen Altertum* (Freiburg, 1931, = *Römische Quartalschrift Supplementheft*, 28).

Greek version of the Pachomian Rule (the original is in Coptic), Pachomius and his disciples had a certain impact on early monasticism in the Western Church, especially in Italy

3

In the World of the Fathers: Palestine, Syria, Cappadocia

Palestine

Palestinian monasticism owes a good deal to Egypt to which, of course, it was geographically close.[1] Areas like Sinai and the Gaza strip, which soon acquired monastic settlements, belong almost equally to both regions. The intercourse between Egypt and Palestine is something we have noted already. In the generation after Anthony, Cassian and his companion, monks of a Bethlehem coenobium, spent much of their time in Egypt on what we might call nowadays 'in-service training'. Furthermore, two of our main narrative sources for Egyptian monasticism – Palladius's 'Lausiac History', composed for the edification of a civil servant, Lausias the Chamberlain, and the anonymous 'History of the Monks' or 'History of the Monks in Egypt', *Historia Monachorum in Aegypto*, were written or, at any rate in the latter case, translated by Western monks with connexions to monasteries on the Mount of Olives.

Travel could also go in the other direction. One way monastic life began in Palestine was through monks with

---

[1] For an overview, see J. Binns, 'Introduction', *Lives of the Monks of Palestine by Cyril of Scythopolis* (Kalamazoo, MI, 1991).

Egyptian experience settling there, a process under way before the death of Anthony. Monks immigrating into Palestine could well say they had found inspiration in biblical forebears, notably Elijah and John the Baptist, both of whose lives have eremitical aspects, and both of whom, of course, lived in the Holy Land. (In the prologue to his life of Paul of Thebes, conventionally the 'first hermit', Jerome treats Elijah and the Baptist as respectively the Old Testament and Inter-Testamental patron saints of the monastic life.) But quite apart from any association with these figures, Palestinian monasticism had some distinctive features worthy of note.

First and foremost, Palestinian monasticism is a very international monasticism. This at once distinguishes it from Egyptian, which seems to have attracted comparatively few foreigners. This internationalism is largely to be explained by the proximity of the Holy Places, and notably what its principal British historian, Derwas Chitty, called 'the Cities of the Incarnation': meaning by that Bethlehem and Jerusalem.[2] In other words, it followed on the popularity of cross-Christendom pilgrimage.[3] The Mount of Olives was an especially favoured site for *coenobia*, owing, Chitty thinks, to the way it provided a view both onto Jerusalem and out towards the desert thus combining, as he puts it, time and eternity. This was in sharp contrast, however, to the Palestinian lavras, hollowed out as these typically were from the side of ravines in the Jordan valley and elsewhere. The internationalism of Palestinian monasticism might be said to prefigure the emergence in the second millennium of brotherhoods that were of set purpose international, such as Mount Athos in the East and the Orders of friars in the West. At any rate it shows a monasticism which is not simply and in every sense within a local church, as, for instance, a Pachomian monastery would

---

[2] D. J. Chitty, *The Desert a City*, op. cit., p. 48.
[3] E. D. Hunt, *Holy Land Pilgrimage in the Later Roman Empire, A.D. 312–460* (Oxford, 1982); P. W. L. Walker, *Holy City, Holy Places: Christian Attitudes to Jerusalem and the Holy Land in the Fourth Century A.D.* (Oxford, 1990).

be, but in some way manifests the Church universal, thus adding a different dimension.

A second difference from the world of the desert fathers was that the Palestinian monasteries, including the lavras in the less populated and more inaccessible areas, had by and large a different view of the relation between the eremitical and coenobitic lives than that which prevailed in Egypt.

In Egypt, the increasing predominance of *coenobia* over against the eremitical settlements was often, if not always, unsought. Though, as Cassian's *Institutes* imply, considerations of prudence on the part of monks themselves played a role in this development,[4] the eventual predominance of the coenobitic life in Egypt was mainly the result of turbulence in the wider world. As early as the fifth century, barbarians from the borderlands of the empire were raiding the monastic settlements, leaving casualties in their wake. Eremitical groups reacted by building high enclosure walls, with just a few anchorites remaining outside. In the seventh century, the Muslim conquest of Egypt intensified this process. Something similar happened on Mount Sinai where the Arabs insisted on the conversion to Islam of local tribes who had formerly protected the occupants of hermitages. So many Egyptian hermits became coenobites for the most prosaic of human reasons: basic security for life and limb.

In Palestine, however, what seems to have been the dominant theory held from the start was that no monk ought to venture on the hermit life unless he had spent some considerable time in a community first, even if that were only a lavra rather than a full-fledged coenobium. A neophyte monk should be trained by others (in the plural) and his vocation more fully discerned. Thus an influential fifth-century figure, the Abba Isaias, who, though an anchorite, founded a coenobitic monastery in the Gaza strip for which he also provided an abbot, warned against the danger of taking up a solitary life

---

[4] Cassian, *Institutes*, VIII, 18.

without sufficient preparatory training in the common life. This did not mean he undervalued the hermit life. Like Cassian, he regarded it as, in principle, a higher calling. Neither life was easy. Community life could be trying and, therefore, a source of growth in the ascetic virtues was needed because the self would encounter yet more demands in solitude, in what he termed the 'cell of quiet'.[5]

The same basic idea, that the coenobium is an essential preliminary stage to the hermitage, is also found in the two most influential monastic founders in the Jordan wilderness, St Euthymius and his disciple St Sabas, whose monasteries, perched high on rocky terraces above the river Jordan opposite Jericho, still survive today, with outlying cave-type houses for hermits. 'Young applicants', so Bishop Kallistos Ware writes in this connexion, 'were not admitted immediately to the lavra but sent to a special coenobium established for novices; after being tested in the common life they might then be allowed to have a cell on their own in the lavra'.[6] And my old Oxford tutor continues with a very nice citation from a near-contemporary *Life*: 'Sabas tells John the Hesychast, "Just as the blossom precedes the fruit, the coenobitic life precedes the anachoretic"'.[7] The larger settlements were major sources of candidates for the episcopate in the East and one of them, the monastery of St Sabas, had a great impact on the development of the Byzantine Liturgy.

Syria

Further north and east from Palestine lies Syria. Here we are not concerned so much with Greek-speaking Syria, the coastal

---

[5] For his teaching, see D. J. Chitty, *The Desert a City*, op. cit., pp. 75–76.
[6] K. T. Ware, 'Separated from all and United to all. The Hermit Life in the Christian East', in A. M. Allchin (ed.), *Solitude and Communion. Papers on the Hermit Life* (Oxford, 1977), p. 38.
[7] Ibid., citing Cyril of Scythopolis, *Life of John the Hesychast*, 6.

region where monasticism resembled the more austere variety of Egyptian anchoritism, but, rather, inland Syriac-speaking Syria, further east. The doctrinal background was complicated by the disputes over the person and nature (natures) of Christ which marred the fifth Christian century. Both in Egypt and Palestine, monks were divided by the disagreements over how to think about the union of divine and human in the Incarnation. They split into Chalcedonian (favouring two distinct natures in Christ after the union) and Monophysite factions (favouring two natures in the moment of the union but one – a divine nature incorporating human properties – after the union). In Syria, the situation was even more confused, since there one could find monks divided into three communions: Chalcedonian, Monophysite, and Nestorian (favouring not only two natures after the union but two persons, the Word and the 'man assumed', whom the union joined). These controversies sundered many Syrian monks from the Great Church, the Church of orthodoxy, or, as we would say, the 'Catholic Church'.

There was another reason too why the Syrian monastic experience was not so well known as it deserved to be. The Syriac language, in which the great majority of non-Chalcedonian Syrian Christian texts are written, was unfamiliar to students in the West until at least the seventeenth century, which was when the papacy ordered the production of Syriac fonts for use by its printing-press. But despite these reasons for thinking of the Syrian monks as a faraway people of whom we know nothing, their monasticism is of considerable interest, not least to Religious in the Latin Church.

There are two reasons for saying this. First, the Syrians provide further theological explanations of the Religious life, and these are worthy of integration into our own. Secondly, even though the most celebrated Syrian monks are the 'pillar-monks' or 'stylites' – the most sedentary ascetics imaginable – the way of life of some monks in this highly diversified monasticism could be said to anticipate the itinerant lifestyle of the friars in the mediaeval West, and thus of other 'clerks regular' who followed the example the friars had set.[8] Let's look now at each of those considerations – the theology and the practice – in turn.

a. Theology

First, then, in their theological reflection, the Syrians are much clearer than any of the sources we have encountered so far about the Christological basis of monasticism, and about, too, its foundation in the sacramental life of the Church, especially Baptism. To this we can add, still under the rubric of 'theology', the Syrians' noteworthy 'angelological' account of Religious life. So first a Christological explanation, to do with the mystery of Christ's person; next an ecclesiological explanation in terms of the sacrament of Baptism; thirdly, an explanation that brings in the angels.

i. The Christological rationale

There is in Syrian monasticism an attempt to give the Religious life a Christological rationale. The Syriac word for a monk, *ihidaya*, translates in the first instance the Greek *monachos*, meaning someone who lives the ascetic, unmarried life: someone who is, as we say in ordinary English, 'single' though by contrast with ordinary English this Greek word also carries the sense of 'single-minded' or 'single-hearted', which makes it highly suitable for expressing St Paul's concept of virginity. But in addition to serving as the equivalent of *monachos*, *ihidaya* also translates a Greek word from a very different context, so far as Christianity is concerned, and this is *monogenês*, 'only-begotten', which is the term in the gospels for Jesus as the Father's only Son.

---

[8] A. Vööbus, *History of Asceticism in the Syrian Orient. A Contribution to the History of Culture in the Near East* (Louvain, 1958–1988, 3 vols.); E. R. Hambye, 'La chiesa siriaca, il suo monachesimo e le loro testimonianze', *Studi francescani* 67 (1970), pp. 295–308.

For the Syrians, religiously motivated celibacy is a matter of a distinctive conformation to Christ. Like Christ, the life of the monk is invested in a unique relation with the Father. The ascetics 'put on' Christ – are intimately joined to him – in a special fashion. Reporting an *agraphon* (an 'unwritten saying' of Jesus, i.e. one that doesn't appear in the gospels but has some claim to be authentic): 'Where there is a single disciple there I shall be equally', St Ephrem the Syrian comments that Christ said this so as

> to remove from the solitaries all cause for sadness, for he is indeed our joy and he is with us.[9]

This provides a much deeper spiritual foundation for the notion of singleness, even singleness of heart, than could the Greek word for a monk when taken in isolation.

ii. The ecclesiological rationale

Then, secondly, the Syrians have an ecclesiological account of Religious life, based, as already mentioned, on holy Baptism. For a period of some time in the Syrian Church, candidates for Baptism were expected to commit themselves to a life of celibacy, prayer, and what would now be called lay ministry. In the homilies of one Syriac teacher, Aphraates, we read:

> The trumpeters, the heralds of the Church, should cry and warn the entire community of God before Baptism, those who have offered themselves for virginity and for holiness.[10]

Candidates who baulked at this and wished to continue conjugal relations with their spouses, were generally enrolled among the Church's members but only as catechumens.

---

[9] Ephrem Syrus, *Commentary on the Diatessaron* 14, 24.
[10] Aphraates, *Demonstrations* 7, 20. Cf. F. C. Burkitt, *Early Eastern Christianity* (London, 1904), p. 125; S. P. Brock, 'Early Syrian Asceticism', *Numen* 20 (1973), pp. 1–19; R. Murray, 'The Exhortation to Candidates for Ascetical Vows at Baptism in the Ancient Syrian Church', *New Testament Studies* 21 (1974), pp. 59–80.

In other words, the monastic way was regarded as the normative expression of baptismal vows, the expected flowering of baptismal grace.¹¹ Monks were referred to as 'sons of the Covenant' (again, the parallel with Qumran is illuminating) and so members *par excellence* of the Church.¹²

iii. An angelological rationale
Finally, there was in Syria an angelological account of religious life. Monks were described as 'those who stand' which meant, in the first instance, stand up for Christ at their Baptism. But the Syriac sources find here a connexion with the angels. In Syriac literature the angels are often called 'watchers', who never sit or sleep and, in this sense, then, they *stand* for the reason that their life is ceaseless praise. This was an idea taken from Judaism. But the Christian Religious is also called to continual prayer. So the life of the monk is an 'angelic' life. The monk shares in the assembly not only of the Church but also of the angels, or perhaps we might say of the one assembly which is both human and angelic.¹³ The Church is traditionally said to be invisible as well as visible. It includes the heavenly Church, or the heavenly Church includes it.

From this it seems to follow that the monk can celebrate a liturgy which is modelled on that of the angels, even when he is not in or even near a church building. In other words, he can celebrate God in the prayer of the heart. This is quite fitting since the earliest Syrian treatise on the Church, the *Liber graduum*, speaks of a perpetual Liturgy taking place in the temple of the heart.

---

[11] A. Vööbus, *Celibacy. A Requirement for Admission to Baptism in the Early Syrian Church* (Stockholm, 1951).
[12] G. Nedungatt, SJ, 'The Covenanters of the Early Syrian speaking Church', *Orientalia Christiana Periodica* 39 (1973), pp. 191–213 and 419–444.
[13] See for this theme K. S. Frank, '*Angelikos bios*'. *Begriffsanalytische und Begriffsgeschichtliche Untersuchung zum 'engelgleichen Leben' im frühen Mönchtum* (Münster, 1994).

So the Syrians have a theologically rich account of what the Religious life is: Christological, baptismal (and therefore sacramental and thus ecclesiological), and also angelological.

b. Practice

The second reason for taking an interest in Syrian monasticism is the way it anticipates in certain respects the friars of the high mediaeval West and the later forms of Religious life that followed on them. Not only were many Syrian monks town-dwellers, whereas no Egyptian monk would have stayed in Alexandria a minute longer than he had to, while their early Palestinian brethren liked to look at the Cities of the Incarnation rather than actually dwell in them. More than this: living, as they did, by a highly interiorised monasticism (compare the *Liber graduum*) with a high theological motivation (Christological, ecclesiological, angelological), it was comparatively easy for the Syrians to become missionaries and practise itinerancy. So Syrian monasticism had a flexibility that enabled it to serve the wider mission of the Church. Like the virgins of the Apocalypse, its monastics followed the Lamb wherever he took them. This was especially true of monks in the Nestorian tradition who carried their version of Christianity to India, central Asia, and finally to China.

Friars such as the Dominicans would retain more of the apparatus of a claustral life, thanks especially to their links through the canons regular with Augustinian monasticism. But they would also be found outside their cloisters, in the service of the Gospel and the Church. Dominican itinerancy could involve complete uprooting, like the migrant Syrians. This was the case with missions to exotic places, which was unusual in the Middle Ages, but far more common in the sixteenth century and later. The normal pattern of Dominican itinerancy was, however, going out from and returning to a base, a priory where a studious and liturgical version of the coenobitic life was lived, and there one refuelled for the next expedition.

Cappadocia

After Palestine and Syria, Cappadocia. It looks as if the Syrians – by their flexibility and their emphasis on how Religious life can serve the wider mission of the Church – may have influenced the monasticism of one of St Benedict's chief approved sources. That source is St Basil, Basil the Great, who lived not in Syria itself but further north, in the district of Anatolia called Cappadocia. (In modern day political terms, this could be described as east-central Turkey.) Though Basilian monasticism, like monasticism everywhere, is primarily contemplative, it also wants to be at the wider service of the Church, defining that service more especially in terms of social concern.[14]

Basil did not begin like this. His early years as an ascetic were spent in what was probably a rather comfortable hermitage, erected on the family estate in what he himself admitted was a lusciously beautiful location, where a wooded valley made its way down to the Black Sea. In letters from this phase of his life, Basil's descriptions of his way of life sound well suited to a Christian intellectual indebted philosophically to the Platonic schools. As we had occasion to note in connexion with Porphyry's life of Plotinus, much of ancient philosophy can be considered a form of spiritual exercise, and so it is here. Basil thinks of contemplation as a purification of the mind – a clarification and focusing of the mind as one moves from the Many to the One, though he marries this philosophical approach with the revealed doctrine of the Psalter, with its advocacy of constant 'remembering' of the God of Israel.[15] Thus in Letter 2 Basil writes:

---

[14] J. Gribomont, 'Saint Basile', in Auctores varii, *Théologie de la Vie monastique. Etudes sur la tradition patristique* (Ligugé, 1961), pp. 99–113.

[15] In his oration to students seeking to combine a classical with a Christian mind-set, Basil recommended the identification of some 'affinity', *oikeiotês*, between the two bodies of teaching, *To the Young Men*, 3. 1.

> Prayer is to be commended, for it engenders in the soul a distinct conception of God. And the indwelling of God is this — to have God set firm within oneself through the process of memory.
>
> We thus become a temple of God whenever earthly cares cease to interrupt the continuity of our memory of him.[16]

But when he was ordained, first as a presbyter and then as bishop of Caesarea (a major See since it was the Cappadocian capital), he came to see things rather differently. Under the impact of these duties, he stressed the need to harness the ascetic movement to meet the Church's wider needs, notably in the philanthropic domain, the realm of practical charity — even if this be at the expense of such intellectual-spiritual contemplation. Sometimes the latter must take second place to pastoral needs.

This wider sense of the needs of the Church is expressed in his first ascetic work, the *Moral Rules*, an arrangement of some 1500 verses of the New Testament. The line he takes here is that the monk must renounce everything worldly because only so will he be able to help the Church effectively in her trials. Of course it could be argued that in some periods the Church's trials are above all intellectual trials, or intellectual-cum-spiritual trials, when contributing to the stabilization of doctrine or making the Christian faith intelligible and credible in the contemporary environment are paramount considerations. Perhaps Basil, who made a major contribution to Trinitarian thinking by his treatise *On the Holy Spirit* which prepared the way for the dogmatization of the divinity of the Spirit at the First Council of Constantinople, would find it difficult totally to disagree.

---

[16] Basil, *Letters*, 2.2, 4, 6. If one accepts that 'remembering God' is biblical as well as Platonic, this letter indicates that 'subtle juxtaposition of Platonism and the Psalms' was not such a 'late achievement' of Basil's as may be thought – e.g. by Philip Rousseau in his *Basil of Caesarea* (Berkeley, CA, and London, [1994] 1998), pp. 82–83.

His other main writings, the *Little Asketikon*, soon translated into Latin, and, from his years as a bishop, the *Great Asketikon*, both of them written in the form of questions-and-answers, and rewritten after his death with altered titles – 'The Shorter Rules' and 'The Longer Rules', became highly influential in the Greek-speaking Church: so much so indeed that insofar as Byzantine monasticism exists in the Eastern Churches united to Rome, it is often referred to in Catholic officialese as 'Basilian' monasticism. These texts, largely from Basil's hand, constitute a combination of asceticism, on the one hand, and a noble Christian humanism on the other. The foundation of his teaching is always the primacy of charity, the love of God and of neighbour: together and inseparably.[17]

For Basil, it is precisely the inseparability of these precepts which should exclude the eremitical life, taken in its radical sense,[18] since the hermit cannot practice fraternal charity. The question Basil puts to the would-be hermit is, 'Whose feet will you wash?'[19] Appropriately, then, Basil and his followers founded coenobitic monasteries that also served as *inter alia* orphanages, hospitals and hostels for the poor. Appropriately, too, the term Basil prefers for a monastery is a 'brotherhood', *adelphotês*. Each brotherhood has an abbot, but the obedience practised is chiefly the reciprocal obedience of all the brothers to each other.

Much of this sounds like some of Augustine but what, surprisingly, we do not seem to find in Basil's writings is the idea that the coenobitic life recreates the *vita apostolica*, the ideal community of the Jerusalem Church. Making that

---

[17] W. R. Lowther Clarke (tr.), *The Ascetic Works of Saint Basil* (London, 1925). An overall interpretation is found in A. Holmes, *A Life Pleasing to God. The Spirituality of the Rules of St Basil* (London, 2000).

[18] I add this qualifying phrase out of respect for St Gregory Nazianzen's report that St Basil allowed hermitages to be built near his coenobia, thus reconciling (in Gregory's view) the two life-ways. Thus Gregory Nazianzen, *Orations*, 43, 62.

[19] Basil, *Longer Rules*, 7, 4.

explicit was, rather, the contribution of the Pachomians and, above all, Augustine. In the Latin Middle Ages, Augustinian canons not only entertained an ecclesial, and notably 'Jerusalem Church'-oriented, theology and spirituality of the common life. They also emulated the Basilian model by running numerous small schools, hospitals and places of retirement for the sick and the aged, as well as for pregnant women, for the blind and for lepers.[20] After the Reformation, many early-modern and modern Congregations of Religious in the West would specialise in one or another of such spiritual or temporal works of mercy – an idea taken up in the Orthodox world only on the eve of the Bolshevik Revolution. As in the twentieth century the modern welfare State advanced into more and more areas of education and philanthropy, these new Institutes of Religious life often seemed to find themselves superfluous, at least in Western Europe and North America. The sentence of doom pronounced on this sort of modern Congregation may, however, be based on a misunderstanding: it is always good for monastics to give witness in suchlike areas, and there ought to be a distinctive quality about it when they do so. Asking whether civil society has no other options available is putting the wrong question.

It may seem surprising that one of the great doctors of the Eastern Church should have wanted the inhabitants of monasteries to get their hands dirty in simple tasks of practical caring. It surprised Basil's great friend and collaborator in the dogmatic struggles of the fourth century, another Cappadocian, Gregory Nazianzen, known in the Greek East as 'The Theologian'. When Basil tried to get Gregory to join one of his foundations, Gregory replied that the intellectual labour of study and argumentation on which he was engaged was an equally demanding kind of labour, worthy to be the daily

---

[20] M. Dunn, *The Emergence of Monasticism. From the Desert Fathers to the Early Middle Ages* (Oxford, 2000), p. 248.

occupation of one who also considered himself a monk.[21] Scholarly Benedictines (like, historically, the Congregation of St Maur), Dominicans, who (with the exception of their lay-brothers) replaced manual labour by study, and no doubt many others, are obliged to take Gregory Nazianzen's side, rather than Basil's, in this dispute.

---

[21] J. A. McGuckin, *St Gregory of Nazianzus. An Intellectual Biography* (Crestwood, NY, 2001), pp. 93–99.

4

In the World of the Fathers: Latin Monasticism, and Notably St Augustine

The wider scene

We move now into the area of Latin monasticism and to its first rule, that of St Augustine. We've already seen how the writings of Cassian, which were composed, significantly, at the request of interested bishops in southern Gaul, suggest the development of anchoritic asceticism into a more structured movement capable of influencing the wider Church. Though the hermit life will never die out completely in the Western Church, and for periods – especially in the so-called Dark Ages – was probably numerically the dominant form of Religious life, the future, so far as Latin Christianity was concerned, lay far more with a corporate monasticism, even if this built on the foundations of proto-monastic asceticism, as had happened in the East at an earlier time.

Though, for its great influence in later centuries, Augustine's Rule and the wider vision it represented deserves special treatment, it would not be right to overlook the role of pre-Augustinian asceticism and monasticism in early Latin Christianity. Not only did individuals follow an ascetic ideal (here aristocratic ladies in Rome seem disproportionately prominent), but many Christians joined hermit groups, notably in island settings which provided both a degree of isolation and yet, in a sea-borne age, allowed for accessibility as well. Examples are Gallinaria, Capraria, and Lérins, the latter the cradle of numerous episcopal vocations. Eastern rules were circulating in Latin translation. Ambrose knew of a Latin version of a Basilian rule; Jerome produced a Latin version of the Rule of Pachomius. Cassian's *Institutes* could be described as of Eastern provenance, though the inspiration had passed through a Latinate lens. Above all, if it is 'light from the East' we are looking for, the eye would turn to Marmoutiers on the Loire, where St Martin of Tours, who had been in the East and was inspired by Hilary of Poitiers, established what can be called the first Western monastery on strictly Eastern lines. But none of those would be, in the long run, so important as the monasticism of Augustine of Hippo.

Augustine's journey

After what is often called his 'moral conversion', dated to 386, when, as he explains in the *Confessions*, he began to lead a chaste life, Augustine's initial steps were somewhat halting. With some Christian friends – rather well-to-do men, highly educated, a number of them married and some, like himself, still catechumens – he set up a form of common life of a studious kind in a villa, with a surrounding estate, in northern Italy: Cassiciacum. It took its cue from high-minded pagan philosophy, and consisted in a search for wisdom through study and discussion, though there was also a serious attempt at growth in the other (moral rather than intellectual) virtues, as well.

This first effort did not survive Augustine's discovery of the exploits of Anthony and the other Egyptian fathers who gave him a desire for a far more radical and stripped-down asceticism, the dedicated virginity of radical – and not least, frugal – discipleship. In comparison, the way of life at Cassiciacum must have seemed far too comfortable and elitist. As the ancient historian and patrologist Henry Chadwick has written:

> Augustine saw the monastic movement as a protest against the infiltration into the churches of the secular loves of power, honour, wealth; a defiance of materialist values and disordered sexuality. Monks were there to show the Church that discipline is actually possible, and that the simplicities of the Sermon on the Mount can be acted out.[1]

At the same time, Augustine realised the implications for the common life of the account of the Jerusalem Church in the Acts of the Apostles. This came naturally to him. As a pastor, he was obsessed by unity – the unity of a group, of a diocese, of the Church as a whole – perhaps because, among other reasons, there was so little of it around him.[2]

These two discoveries – the desert fathers and the portrait of the Jerusalem Church in Acts – explain the further evolution of Augustine's efforts at monastic foundation. In 388 he founded, in his parental home at Tagaste in his native North Africa, a community of 'servants of God' which included prayer, fasting and manual labour among its features, as well as study, common life, writing and spiritual colloquy. In 391, now a presbyter at Hippo, he created a 'garden monastery' for lay monks, emphasising renunciation of goods, celibacy, and, at least implicitly, obedience. It was for this monastery that he wrote his Rule. In 395, as bishop of Hippo, he established a monastery of clerics in the bishop's house – clericalising the monastic movement (though he also wished to 'monasticise' clerics by gathering them into communities of this kind). The way of life of members of his monastery now included liturgical celebrations in the bishop's basilica,

---

[1] H. Chadwick, 'The Ascetic Ideal in the History of the Church', in W. J. Shiels, *Monks, Hermits and the Ascetic Tradition*, op. cit., p. 20.
[2] C. W. Brockwell, 'Augustine's Ideal of Monastic Community', *Augustinian Studies* 8 (1977), pp. 91–109. See too A. Zumkeller, *Augustine's Ideal of the Religious Life* (New York, 1986).

preaching, teaching, hospitality and arbitration of cases in the ecclesiastical and civil courts. (Remotely, that is the origin of Augustinian canons, as distinct from Augustinian friars, who originally were hermits but were brought together for mutual assistance in a common life.)

Augustine's doctrine of the monastic life

In his Rule, Augustine opens by declaring that the chief reason the members of a *monasterium* are gathered into one is to live unanimously in the house, having one soul (or 'mind') and one heart intent upon God.[3] Augustine had noticed that for the author of Acts (and not only in his account of the Jerusalem Church), unanimity is a hallmark of the community that carries the Gospel. It is, of course, unanimity in what concerns Christian revelation, not on a host of civil matters where a degree of variability in judgment is a precondition of a healthy public opinion. Obedience to the Word of God means the making of a common mind and, something equally difficult, given the vagaries of human temperament, a common heart. Normally, such unanimity is not publicly possible without authoritarianism among those who rule or hypocrisy among those who are ruled. But for Augustine, a common mind and heart are certainly possible if they are part and parcel of a spiritual moving together towards God. This is a point he conveys so laconically it may easily be overlooked. The one mind and one heart he is speaking of in the Rule are those of people living *in Deum*: meaning not 'in God', which in Latin would be rendered *in Deo*, but, rather, as I translated it, 'intent upon God': keen to hear his voice and attain him. The primitive Dominican Constitutions insist that this unity should be not only internal but external, embodied, when they remark:

---

[3] The best study is G. Lawless, OSA, *Augustine of Hippo and his Monastic Rule* (Oxford, 1987), which also includes a Latin and English text.

> It is right that, as we live under one Rule and by the vow of a single profession, so uniformity of observance should be found in our Order so that the unity kept in our hearts may be fostered and represented by the exterior uniformity kept in our customs.[4]

In Augustine's theology of the monastic life, as found outside the Rule in his wider corpus, the unity of the monastery is, *first*, closely connected with the spiritual perfection at which all asceticism aims, and has, *secondly*, an ecclesiological rationale giving it a special relation to the Church at large. *Thirdly*, the unity of the monastic community has an eschatological rationale, in terms of the ultimate Christian hope. *Fourthly*, and this is something new, it has a special relation to God as Trinity.

First, then, how is unity connected with spiritual perfection? Augustine's answer is, through the concept, and more than the concept, the practice, of charity. One eloquent, if somewhat florid, locus of his teaching along those lines is his discourse on Psalm 132, of which the opening line runs: 'Behold how good and lovely it is, brothers dwelling in unity'. Augustine maintains that anointing by the Holy Spirit under the New Covenant – prefigured in the psalm by the consecratory oil dripping down from the head of Aaron, the prototype Jewish high priest – descends first onto the humanity of Christ, who is our Head, the new Adam, and then onto the apostles – prefigured in the psalm by the oil reaching Aaron's beard, and finally onto the Church which Augustine calls here Christ's 'vestment', so as to have an equivalent for the psalm's statement that the oil ends up 'on the collar of Aaron's robe'. This anointing by the Spirit, or, to put it in a less symbolic manner, the presence and activity of the Holy Spirit, expresses itself, says Augustine, at this third ecclesial level – the level of the Church at large – in the form of charity. It is charity that makes brotherly concord possible in the monastery. And,

---

[4] *Constitutiones antiquae Fratrum Sacri Ordinis Praedicatorum*, Prologue.

likewise, it is charity which is the aim of the ascetical life, and indeed of the moral life, or the Christian life, as a whole.[5] So through the mediating concept, and of course practice, of charity, the unity of the monastery is linked to the goal of the monastic life as such. (Compare this to Pachomius.)

That the unity of the monastery is an example of the impact of the Holy Spirit on the Church at large prepares us for the *second* aspect of Augustine's monastic theology I drew attention to, and that is how, like several of the other figures we have looked at, he finds for Religious life an ecclesiological rationale. A Religious community where the members 'live in the house in unity of spirit' (cf. Psalm 67,7), is a model of the Church because, for Augustine, the Church is a temple or house of God which is formed by living stones, living stones that are 'those who are united by charity'.[6] Incidentally, that was the theme of Pope Benedict XVI's first doctoral thesis, on the Church as house and people of God in Augustine's theology.

Thirdly, Religious life has an eschatological rationale in Augustine, since such a community is also an image of the heavenly City. In Book XV of his treatise *De Civitate Dei*, Augustine, with some assistance from ancient philosophy, seeks to describe the eschatological city by extrapolation from what is said in Scripture of the outcome of the work of the Holy Spirit, but the result is very much like his description of a monastery. Of the 'citizens of the free city, the sharers in eternal peace', he writes that they

> form a community where there is ... a love that rejoices in a good that is at once shared by all and [yet] unchanging – a love that makes one heart out of many, a love that is the wholehearted and harmonious obedience of mutual affection.[7]

---

[5] See the essays in Auctores varii, *La Charité et l'unité. Une clé pour entrer dans la théologie de saint Augustin* (Paris, 1993).
[6] Augustine, *Sermons*, 336, 1.
[7] Idem., *The City of God*, XV. 3.

Fourthly, and finally, there is a Trinitarian aspect to the communitarian life of the Church and thus to the coenobitic life which is the model of the Church and an image of the future City of God, in Augustine's vision. A distinctive feature of Augustine's theology of the triune God is the way in which he portrays the Holy Spirit as the bond of love between the Father and the Son, such that the unity of the Trinity consists not simply in the unity of the divine nature which Father, Son, and Spirit personalise, nor just in the unity conferred by the Father as the source of the other divine persons, but in the unity operated by the Holy Spirit through his unification of the life of the Father and the Son in the charity which he personally is. So, applying this to the monastery, the unity-in-charity of multiple human persons reflects the manner of being of the Trinity itself. Augustine spells this out in his *Tractates on the Gospel of John* where he writes, citing his favourite text from the Acts of the Apostles: 'They were of one soul and one heart towards God' (Acts 4:32). And he comments, 'Listen, brothers, and from this recognise the mystery of the Trinity'.[8]

Precisely because Augustine sees the monastery as the ideal form of the Church, he starts to treat his monasteries, which began as communities of lay ascetics, as specially suited to the life of the clergy. To cite Chadwick again:

> The new monasteries could train men in a frugal life and become nurseries of bishops, who would go out and gather their presbyters around them in a clergy-house, eating and praying regularly together.[9]

Some of Augustine's monasteries were for women. That consideration would obviously not apply in their case. But the quotation has the merit of showing how relatively easy it was for Augustinian monasticism to develop, in the early Middle

---

[8] Augustine, *Tractates on the Gospel of John*, 39, 5.
[9] H. Chadwick, 'The Ascetic Ideal in the History of the Church', art. cit., p. 19.

Ages, into the institution of the canons regular, which, unlike Benedictine monasticism, was a specifically priestly form of religious life,[10] and one quite often lived in close proximity to the house and church of the bishop – for instance here in England at Carlisle, or in Scotland at Whithorn, or in St Dominic's Castile, at Osma.

A summary so far

To summarise: though the motifs of virginity (or celibacy) and the common life are originally distinct, they tend increasingly to converge. That had implications for practice, first of all. Where the themes of virginity and the coenobium converge, the common life is pursued as essentially a life of celibates and even, where the discipline of the cell is prized, of solitaries. Monastics come to regard the common life as a safeguard for celibates, providing them with the means of fraternal correction, or a necessary training ground, or as a way of turning their energies to the service of the Church. We might say that the Religious life is increasingly seen as a life that is simultaneously together and alone: alone by habitual prayer and spiritual reading or study, together by common concord.

This did not mean, however, that the coenobitic life simply incorporated the virginal life into itself. There were those who remained outside the coenobia, either wholly or in part. To remain unmarried for the honour of the Lord could lend itself not only to the fixed, geographically stable life of the hermit, but also to the more mobile, missionary activities of the Syrian solitaries.

And just as there was more than one way for the Church to use the virgin, so too there was more than one way for the Church to understand the point of the common life. It could

---

[10] R. Foreville – J. Leclerq, 'Un débat sur le sacerdoce des moines au XIIe siècle', *Studia Anselmiana* XLI (1957), pp. 117–118.

be valued as an expression of the Church's nature as a communion of charity (Augustine, or, somewhat earlier in the East, Pachomius), or as enabling monks to take on institutionalised works of charity (as with Basil), or as a training ground for future ordained ministers (Augustine again).

Over time, so we saw, the connexions of the Religious life to various aspects of Christian doctrine became more apparent. In Anthony, and among the other desert fathers, the anchoritic life is a providential way to appropriate for oneself the salvation revealed in Scripture. Some desert voices speak of it as a life of intercession for the Christian city. In Pachomius, monasticism is an instrument of the wider divine purpose to reconcile human beings with each other in God. Among the Syrians, the life of the monk is seen as Christomorphic, a plenary living out of the grace of adoptive sonship given in Baptism, as well as an embodiment of the Church that unites humans and angels. In Augustine the monastic community expresses the archetypal Church of the Acts of the Apostles, and by the unity in charity of its plural membership foreshadows the life of the City of God. We could sum this up by saying we are talking about a life with soteriological, Christological, ecclesiological and eschatological dimensions.

From here one could take a further step. In the measure that people become aware of these further dimensions, the realisation dawns that the Religious life is very much a liturgical life, for the Liturgy combines just these four dimensions: soteriological, Christological, ecclesiological, eschatological. It celebrates the mysteries of salvation in the liturgical cycle and makes their content available to us (soteriological). It celebrates Christ as our great high priest, the Mediator between God and man through whom all liturgical prayer is offered, and in so doing brings him before our inner eye (Christological). It celebrates the Church as the beloved spouse of Christ. The voice of the Liturgy is the voice of the Church as his bride (ecclesiological). It also celebrates the messianic banquet in the future, definitive City of God (eschatological). So the way lies open to the strongly liturgical life of the black monks or Benedictines and the equally liturgical life of the canons regular of the early and high Middle Ages.

5

From the Fathers, Especially St Benedict, to the Mediaevals

The coming of St Benedict

It was said in the last chapter that the discovery of the simultaneously soteriological, Christological and ecclesial-sacramental dimensions of the Religious life opened the way to a recognition of its fundamentally liturgical character, since the Liturgy itself has precisely these dimensions. In other words, a fundamental congruence is or should be apparent between the project of monasticism on the one hand, and the celebration of the Liturgy on the other. In a sense, the emergence in the West of Benedictinism is what demonstrates this affinity.

In the patristic developments, the way is prepared for Benedict's statement in his Rule, the most celebrated of the Rules of the West, stemming from the century after Augustine, that nothing is to be preferred to the 'work of God', the *opus Dei*.[1] Ascetics in Rome, where Benedict had had his education, seem to have lived chiefly around the main basilicas, and it is around those churches that the earliest Roman monasteries were founded, starting with the monastery called 'At the

---

[1] The relation of the Benedictine *Regula monachorum* to the nearly contemporary 'Rule of the Master', three times its length but probably also from central Italy, is disputed.

Catacombs' established by Pope Sixtus III, circa 435, by the side of the basilica of St Sebastian on the Appian Way. Roman proto-monasticism is often called 'basilican monasticism', and this is a way of indicating that from the start it was linked to the centres of liturgical cultus.[2] Benedict's day is dominated by the Liturgy of the Hours but his Rule has nothing to say about the Mass, probably because that was under the authority of the bishop, and also because, at the time Benedict was writing, its celebration would have been an affair for Sundays and major feasts only.

But Benedict (c. 480-547) by no means regards a monastery as simply a household devoted to the Liturgy. It is, he says, a 'school of the Lord's service'. Taking 'schola' in its educational sense, that will mean a place to learn wisdom, which could link the Rule with the concept of a learned monasticism, emerging at the same period with Cassiodorus, a Roman aristocrat who founded a monastery along those lines in southern Italy. One historian has written of Cassiodorus' *Institutes* that in them he 'encouraged [the monks of Vivarium] to study profane as well as ecclesiastical authors, to develop their intellectual skills by reading pagan literature as well as the works of the Church fathers'.[3] But most of the Greek texts translated were in fact patristic or canonical rather than literary and, after Cassiodorus' death, this programme for a learned monasticism was gradually abandoned, and the contents of the library of Vivarium dispersed, entering instead the collections of the papacy and, in the far north, the Anglo-Saxon monasteries of Jarrow and Monkwearmouth – a sign that Cassiodorus' picture was not in fact totally obliterated among Religious.

But back to St Benedict. The alternative sense of the word 'schola' in his Rule is military: this was a technical name for an

---

[2] G. Ferrari, *Early Roman Monasteries. Notes for the History of the Monasteries and Convents at Rome, from the VIth through the IXth Centuries* (Vatican City, 1957).

[3] J. Herrin, *The Formation of Christendom*, op. cit., p. 80.

elite corps of the Roman army.[4] In which case, Benedict is speaking about the monk's spiritual warfare, which links him back to Anthony and the desert tradition. Certainly his ascetic doctrine draws on Egyptian sources (Pachomius and Cassian) as well as the Cappadocian experience (Basil). The monk, stresses Benedict, should persevere in one monastery, practising conversion of life under an abbot who is at once spiritual father and administrator. The monk is to seek God, climbing up the steps of humility towards Christian perfection.

After Benedict

But despite this wider spiritual context, the remarks of the Rule about the *opus Dei* were what made the most impression on the late patristic and early mediaeval period. From the ninth century above all, the black monks hold to a *doxological* theology of the Religious life, which reflects the increasing domination of the day by liturgical roles, somewhat at the expense of Benedict's original plan, which is for the subdivision of the day into three more or less equal parts: worship, reading, and manual labour.[5] Historians suggest that the (temporary) victory of this overwhelmingly liturgical understanding of the monastic life was the consequence of two factors, one more important than the other. The first was the ninth-century reform of the Western monasteries, mandated by the Carolingian emperors and spearheaded by St Benedict of Aniane: this provided for a much more elaborate liturgy, including a daily sung conventual Mass, as well as private Masses for ordained monks, the daily Office of the Dead alongside the Great Office, and numerous processions. The

---

[4] C. E. Lawrence, *Medieval Monasticism. Forms of Religious Life in Western Europe in the Middle Ages* (London and New York, 1989, 2nd edition), p. 31.

[5] On Benedictine monasticism, see C. Butler, OSB, *Benedictine Monachism* (London, 1924); B. Steidle, OSB, *The Rule of St Benedict, a Commentary* (Canon City, CO, 1967).

other factor was the transcribing and development of Gregorian chant.

> The idea that the perfect execution of the liturgy was the characteristic function of a Benedictine community originated in the ninth-century reform.[6]

To put it more theologically: Religious life is a wonderful waste of time, giving glory to the God whose own life consists in the ceaseless mutual glorification of the divine persons.

The white monks

Dedication to an increasingly elaborate 'perpetual praise', *laus perennis*, associated above all with the numerous monasteries dependent on the Burgundian abbey of Cluny, had a salutary reaction in the foundation of the Cistercians, the 'white monks', over against the black.[7] In a day so dominated by corporate worship, where was the place for solitude, personal reflection and manual labour – all of which were major monastic concerns in Benedict's sources? The Cistercian reform also expressed a desire to return to the poverty and simplicity of life of early asceticism, instead of the often palatial settings of black monk existence, which contrasted so sharply with the lifestyle of the majority of laypeople, who were peasants in a subsistence economy. The Cistercian 'customs', provisions for the character of the life as lived day by day, influenced the Dominicans via the Premonstratensians.

Predictable in this context is the influence of the Cistercian reform of the chant on the Dominican liturgical books. In each case the signature tune was austere beauty – of life, or of sound. Not that aestheticism has anything to do with it. Essentially, the first Cistercians placed themselves in the school of the ancient monks, seeking to draw on the reserves of grace

---

[6] C. E. Lawrence, *Medieval Monasticism*, op. cit., p. 80.
[7] C. H. Berman, *The Cistercian Evolution. The Invention of a Religious Order in Twelfth-Century Europe* (Philadelphia, 2000).

their example and teaching held. Indeed, all the 'new movements' of the eleventh and twelfth centuries have it in common that they wished to go back to the sources. *Ressourcement* is not a phenomenon of twentieth-century Catholicism alone. In the early mediaeval age, as in late modernity, the hope was to access anew the inspiration of the Church of the Fathers – in this case, the monastic fathers whether of East or of West.

The Cistercians were not the only significant element in the background to the founding of the Dominicans, though we should certainly not overlook the obvious fact that Bishop Diego and St Dominic were consciously continuing the mission of the Cistercian abbots in south-western France to reconvert the Albigensians to the Catholic Church. Diego and Dominic evidently thought they would be more efficacious if they could out-Cistercianise the Cistercians in austerity of life. The most important single element in the background was the reform of the canons regular, but the impressive renewal of the hermit life should not be missed. All these movements: the advent of the Cistercians, the reform of the canons regular, the new Orders of hermits, set the tone for Dominic's religious world. One historian blocks them all together under the title, 'The Quest for the Primitive'. The new hermits and equally new canons deserve a further word.

The new hermits

The new eremitical movements of the twelfth century stressed solitude in communion, and they typically practiced the solitary life with others who were like-minded.[8] The key maxim of the new hermits was 'plural solitude', *solitudo*

---

[8] H. Leyser, 'The New Eremitical Movements in Western Europe, 1000–1150' (D. Phil. thesis, University of Oxford, 1966).

pluralis. The phrase was coined by the eleventh-century monastic reformer St Peter Damian,[9] but it was widely taken up among the Camaldolese and the Carthusians, the two principal new groups.[10] For Peter Damian it implied not just an architectural layout, a practical scheme for a Western version of the Eastern *lavra*, a colony of hermits in adjacent cells. 'Plural solitude' included a whole theological vision of the Church as a unified multitude, a communion, that can be present to and even in a single person, owing to the bonds of charity, notably as exercised through intercession for the entire Mystical Body. And this is in fact (if he is true to his vocation) the hermit's case.

It is not irrelevant to note the white habits adopted by the Camaldolese and the Carthusians who shared Peter Damian's basic idea. The colour of the cloth, or rather its lack of colour ('white' meant made from 'undyed' wool), belongs with the desire to get back to the primitive inspiration: the fundamental imperatives of virginity and simplicity heard as the call of the desert. Peter Damian's doctrine was already there in embryo when the unknown fifth-century author of the *History of the Monks of Egypt* wrote of the Egyptian hermits, 'They are scattered in the desert and in separate cells but they are united in charity'.[11]

The new eremitical Order which, by general agreement, is pertinent to the Dominicans, is one that has now disappeared (it was suppressed in 1772), the Order of Grandmont, founded in central-southern France by Stephen of Muret who died in 1124. It is thought to be significant that the most reliable account of Stephen's life is the one offered by the

---

[9] Explaining why a hermit, when alone, could use in his liturgical prayers the formula 'Dominus vobiscum': see Peter Damian, 'The Book of the Lord Be With You', in Patricia McNulty (tr.), *Peter Damian. Selected Writings* (London, 1959), pp. 53–54.

[10] André Louf, OCSO, 'Solitudo pluralis', in A. M. Allchin (ed.), *Solitude and Communion*, op. cit., pp. 17–29.

[11] Cited in ibid., p. 20.

Dominican Vincent of Beauvais in his *Speculum maius*, 'The Larger Mirror'. Stephen's teaching, given orally, was subsequently written up by Hugh Lacerta, one of his disciples, as the 'Book of Sentences'. Hugh also wrote a 'Way of Life' which aimed to formulate Stephen's basic project.[12] St Dominic's maxim 'to speak only to God or about God' is Grandmontine, and so is his plan to give lay-brothers (what are now called co-operator brothers) responsibility for administering the material goods of the Order. The resistance of the first Dominican General Chapters to this idea may have been stiffened by knowledge of the crisis this division of powers caused for the Grandmontines, necessitating a papal intervention to reassert the primary authority of its clerical monks towards the end of the twelfth century. But the synthesis of solitude and coenobitic life that typifies the new hermits at Grandmont as elsewhere just had to be abidingly pertinent to preaching friars for whom study – inevitably a solitary activity – was a crucial means to the goal.

The new canons

As to the new canons, canons regular have rather a complex history. Basically, they are at the point of confluence of two streams. First, they are the result of attempts by bishops, who themselves were committed to the ascetic life, to group their presbyters into communities of a quasi-monastic kind. We have seen how Augustine of Hippo exemplifies that trend. Secondly, they derive from a certain unwillingness on the part of non-Benedictine monastics to embrace a purely Benedictine ideal. When the Carolingian monarchy sought, through Benedict of Aniane, to impose the Rule of the original St Benedict on coenobitic monasteries, a number of monasteries,

---

[12] M. Wilkinson, 'The Vita Stephani Muretensis and the Early Life of Stephen of Muret', in J. Loades (ed.), *Monastic Studies. The Continuity of Tradition* (Bangor, 1990), pp. 102–127.

which previously had been eclectic in their choice of inspiration, preferred to redefine themselves in terms of the *ordo canonicus* instead.

Outside the Carolingian empire the same sort of process might occur for other reasons. For example, in the British Isles, houses of monks coming from a Celtic Church background in Scotland and Ireland could end up as houses of canons as part of a process of a more thorough integration into the ways of the European Church. Colonies of hermits might follow suit, though not necessarily with the same motivation. Thus in the eleventh century a group of hermits were living at Llanthony near the Welsh-English border. By 1120 they had become a house of 'Austin canons', seeking no doubt the greater stability that belonging to the 'canonical order' conferred.[13] Speaking generally: that 'order' consisted of *clerics vowed to asceticism* in contra-distinction to the 'monastic order' which consisted, rather, of *ascetics, some of whom would be ordained*. Priesthood was essential to the canons regular: they pursued priestly perfection by means of monastic asceticism.

A number of different documents could be taken to set out the principles of the canonical life, but by the eleventh century the Rule of Augustine had emerged as overwhelmingly the preferred text. The Rule was now reinterpreted in a new context, compared with its fifth-century origins. It was a rule for priests and other clerics who saw themselves as *deputati ad chorum*, dedicated to the choral celebration of the Mass and the Hours as an oblation of praise, supplication and thanksgiving on behalf of the whole Church. Even though canonical houses did not allow the Liturgy to elbow out time for other things, still, the regular canon considered himself to have no higher office than to worship representatively on behalf of the Church. Of course, for any follower of the Rule of Benedict the Liturgy was 'the work of God' par excellence. Yet because

---

[13] J. Dickinson, *The Origin of the Austin Canons* (London, 1949), pp. 111–112.

communities of canons are essentially communities of priests (though they may have lay-brothers as auxiliaries), the rhythmic division of the day by the Liturgy of the Hours is seen by them as an 'official' act – from which we get the phrase 'Officium divinum'. Unlike monks, they are the official representatives of the Church.

Most houses of regular canons comprised priests concerned with pastoral ministry in their vicinity, but some, such as the celebrated French abbey of St Victor, just outside Paris, were far more contemplative and intellectual in orientation than they were pastoral. Intellectually-minded clerics trained in the University schools were sometimes attracted to the more contemplative version of the academic priesthood represented by the canons regular whose typical study-life bridged the gap between the older patristic and monastic theology on the one hand, and the new dialectics of argumentative Scholasticism on the other. In time, such clerics would also look to the Dominicans: the career of Jordan of Saxony, patron of Dominican vocations, revolves around this.[14] Thomas Aquinas is more Scholastic than the Victorines but he has by no means left behind the Fathers and monastic theologians like Cassian and Bernard.

Many houses of regular canons were very small, and the attempt of the Fourth Lateran Council to get them to coordinate in at least a loose federation of Austin Canons was unsuccessful. Probably that is why so many of these foundations eventually disappeared. What could and did succeed, however, were particular congregations of houses. Of these, by far the most important were the Premonstratensians. The division between houses of regular canons that were primarily engaged in an active ministry on the one hand, and those that were more contemplative on the other, is graphically represented by the Premonstratensians, founded by St Norbert of

---

[14] M. Aron, *St Dominic's Successor* (London, 1955).

Cologne in the 1120s.[15] Norbert intended his white canons to be not only pastoral but missionary in orientation, but from the basis of a liturgical common life of a strongly ascetic kind. So they were in eastern Germany, which is where he founded them as archbishop of Magdeburg in a missionary territory. But in much of the rest of Europe, Premonstratensian abbeys had no mission field, and often no pastoral responsibilities of an institutional kind. As a consequence, the German abbeys often argued their loyalty lay more to successive archbishops of Magdeburg than to the General Chapter of Prémontré. As one historian puts it:

> The full realisation of Norbert's vision of a canonical order following a monastic regime, but committed to an active missionary understanding of the *vita apostolica*, had to await the coming of the Dominican friars in the thirteenth century.[16]

With Norbert, the phrase 'apostolic life', which had earlier meant a coenobitic life modelled on the Jerusalem community of Acts, adds an extra connotation without losing the earlier one. It is a life of apostolic mission through the ministry of the Word to pagans, the ministry of the Word and sacraments to the converted. Not surprisingly, someone (Brian Farrelly) has called Norbert the grandfather of the Dominicans.

'Orders' arrive

As well as austerity of life, the new Orders who answered the call to the primitive had something else in common which they would pass on to the Dominicans, and this was a coordinated system of government on an international level. Though this has some roots in Cluniac monasticism, it was only half-

---

[15] F. Petit, *La spiritualité des Prémontrés aux XIIe et XIIIe siècles* (Paris, 1947); B. Ardura, *Prémontrés. Histoire et spiritualité* (Saint-Etienne, 1995). Their maxims were: 'the praise of God in choir', 'Eucharistic cultus', 'the cultus of Mary', 'the spirit of the yoke of penance', 'zeal for souls'.
[16] C. E. Lawrence, *Medieval Monasticism*, op. cit., p. 172.

hearted there. It gets off the ground with the Cistercians, the Carthusians, the Premonstratensians and then, in their wake, the Dominicans and the other Orders of friars. All of these are Orders with a single supreme legislative body, the General Chapter. All have a simple system of affiliation and visitation affecting every house of the Order. All such Orders are exempted in many respects from episcopal control, something which the emergence of a stronger papacy had made possible in the Gregorian reform of the eleventh century. All insist, at any rate in principle, on uniformity of practice in their houses. In the words of one mediaevalist:

> The Cistercians achieved at one stroke the kind of organization every ruler would wish to have: a system complete in itself, wholly autonomous, equipped with a thorough organization for internal supervision, isolated from external interference, untroubled by those sources of dispute about services and rights which choked the law courts of Europe. The Cistercian system was the first effective International organization in Europe, more effective even than the papal organization because it had narrower aims and a smaller field of operation.[17]

With this topic of government, we have covered virtually everything that can be regarded as constitutive in the history and theology of Religious life. All subsequent Religious life, not least Dominican life, will draw on the different practices, structures and themes already mentioned, but in various ways suggested by changing epochs, cultures, circumstances, needs in the Church. Leaving aside the question of international organisation, which was a contribution of the high Middle Ages, we can say that the main practical features of the historic Religious life and the chief themes in a theology of Religious

---

[17] R. W. Southern, *Western Society in the Middle Ages* (Harmondsworth, 1970), p. 255. 'At one stroke' is, however, too strong: the emergence of an *ordo cisterciensis* was a more improvised affair (compare the study by Constance Berman, note 7 above).

life, are a gift from the patristic period, the age of the Fathers of the Church.

If there is an exception to that statement it could be the existence of a systematic theology of the Religious life for which St Thomas Aquinas provides the model. That would centre on a theology of vows – not surprisingly because, from towards the end of the patristic period, vows came to take on that major importance which doctrinally, spiritually and canonically they hold today. Thomas also begins to reflect about the rationale of there being no longer simply monasticism in general but a plurality of Religious Orders with missions that differ. So that will be our next topic.

6

The Common Doctor: St Thomas Aquinas on the Religious Life

A state of perfection?

Reflecting on the elements of practice and theory that came down to him, Thomas tries to provide a systematic theology of the Religious life. St Thomas's notion of what such a theology should be is focussed on the idea of perfection – to be precise, *evangelical* perfection, the kind of perfection Jesus wanted for his disciples when he said, 'Be perfect, as your heavenly Father is perfect' (Matthew 5:48). This is the perfection for whose sake he counselled the rich young man in Matthew 19:21 – 'if you would be perfect, go, sell what you possess and give to the poor, and you will have treasure in heaven, and come, follow me'. Follow him, that is, by a life of simple discipleship. We saw how, in the Gospels, at least when read in terms of a trajectory into the early Church, such a life is envisaged as, on the one hand, a life of consecrated virginity and, on the other, a common life with fellow disciples. These are the motifs that come together in the beginnings of the monastic institution, taking different though inter-related forms in the various kinds of Religious life known to the Church of the first centuries.

In Greek, the word for 'perfection', *teleiôsis*, and the word for 'goal', *telos*, are related, and so, in ascetical theology, talk about becoming perfect as a disciple was quickly related to talk of reaching one's goal as a Christian and, insofar as supernature subsumes nature, as a human being too. St Thomas's vocabulary of 'perfection' seeks to express this. For a Christian, whose nature has been remade by grace – at least in principle, in its foundation ('If anyone is in Christ', wrote St Paul, 'he is a new creation' [II Corinthians 5:17]), that will be a matter of giving perfect expression to the grace-life which is now second nature to us – the life of sanctifying grace implanted in us by Baptism – and in that way coming to our goal.

St John Cassian – as important a source for Thomas as for Dominic – had defined that goal as purity of heart leading to the vision of God, though, owing to his debt to Augustine and behind Augustine to the evangelist John, Thomas prefers to speak here of *charity* leading to such union. Perfect charity is what purity of heart most deeply consists in.

In his theology of what a Religious is, Thomas's most characteristic focus is to describe the life of the monk or nun, hermit, friar, canon regular (or whatever other terms are used) as the inhabiting of what he calls a 'state of perfection'. This phrase has sometimes been misunderstood, so it is as well to be clear at the outset what he means by it. For Thomas, a state of perfection is a form of life which, if one corresponds to what it represents, necessarily brings one to the kind of perfection the Gospel speaks of.

Thomas introduces this approach in a typically careful and thorough way. He begins by enquiring first what a state of life is before, in the second place, going on to apply this concept to the Church and monasticism, when he will discuss why it is appropriate to have more than one state of life in the Church as well as what is entailed by the state that he calls the 'state of perfection'.

So then, what, in the most general terms, does Aquinas mean by a 'state'? For Thomas, a 'state' (*status*) is a stable form of life in which human freedom is committed and used in a certain way. This emphasis on freedom in saying what

Religious life is all about almost certainly derives from St Bernard. His privileging of freedom, part and parcel of the so-called humanism of the twelfth century, is signalled in the way he gives to freedom the crucial role in man's imaging of God that earlier in the Latin tradition St Augustine had given to intellect.[1] Defining the Christian life as a state in which freedom is existentially engaged, then, Thomas goes on to argue that it is only appropriate that in the Church there should be a number of such states. It takes a variety of states in the Church in order to manifest that overflowing fullness of life which, as he puts it, is in God 'simply and uniformly'.[2] It also makes for a harmonious fulfilment of the different purposes the Church has on earth. As usual, Thomas is sparing of examples, but we could think, for instance, of the obvious contrast between the state of life of the hermit, witnessing to the ultimate divine vocation of humanity to be united with God, absorbed in him, and the state of life of the Christian statesman called to influence the temporal affairs of this world in ways that assist its integral human and divine fulfilment.

Such contrasts are not for Thomas merely functional, though they are also that. Over and above the functional, they have a significance on the level of what would now be termed 'theological aesthetics'. The co-existence of different states in the Church is directed to the Church's perfection in the sense of her splendid manifestation of the plenitude of the grace which inheres in her divine-human Head, Jesus Christ. It enhances what Thomas calls the dignity and beauty of the Church, which beauty consists in a certain orderedness of (corporate) life.[3]

Refining his analysis, Thomas remarks that the diversity among Christ's faithful is on three levels. First, such diversity is

---

[1] E. Gilson, *L'Esprit de la philosophie médiévale* (Paris, 2008 [1960]), p. 217.
[2] Thomas Aquinas, *Summa theologiae* IIa. IIae., q. 183, a. 2, corpus.
[3] Ibid.

a matter of differences of state, such that some states are more perfect than others. Secondly, that diversity comes from the different sorts of action required by the various offices or tasks – the diverse sets of duties – which the Church must, through her members, fulfil. Granted that Christians do, then, occupy different states, and have different tasks as well, it is also the case – thirdly – that even within the same state and the same office people are at different stages, operating on different levels. In all states there are people who are beginning, people who are advancing, and people who are reaching perfection.

In Thomas's Latin, there are *incipientes, proficientes et perficientes*, and these words have a very ancient origin.[4] They reflect the Greek of the sixth-century Syrian monk Denys the Areopagite's treatise 'On the Ecclesiastical Hierarchy', behind which is the ethical vocabulary of the Neo-Platonist philosophers who influenced Denys. For some commentators, chiefly Protestant, any drawing by Christian theology on pagan philosophers is worrying. But, even aside from the fact that this particular Platonist distinction is surely anodyne, the general approach of the Catholic tradition has been to say that, quite to the contrary, theology needs philosophy in order to increase theology's own power of thought.

So far Thomas has been talking about perfection in a very formal kind of manner. He has not yet come to terms with its material content. Actually, then, or concretely, in what does Christian perfection consist? Thomas's reply is that the perfection of the Christian life consists principally in the charity which unites us to God as our final end.[5] So the question then becomes, Can anyone have perfect charity in this life? Thomas replies that it must be so, because the divine law does not command the impossible, yet the Word incarnate said, 'Be perfect as your heavenly Father is perfect' (Matthew 5:48). Here, however, with his customary realism,

---

[4] Ibid., a. 4.
[5] Ibid., q. 184, a. 1.

Thomas introduces a distinction. For the one who loves God to love him absolutely, totally, such that his love for God is exercised at all times, and in its full capacity, is only possible in heaven. What is possible on earth is a kind of perfection which excludes everything that would be contrary to the love of God, not only every mortally sinful action or omission in deed, word, or thought (even beginners in the way of Christian perfection, according to Aquinas, should manage that), but also 'whatever would prevent the affection of the soul from being directed totally to God'.[6] It should be possible to avoid everything which would prevent the soul's affection going straight to God, prevent it through involvement with attachment to good things in the created order, things which can in practice behave not only as media through which to love God but as centres of attraction that are an alternative to him.

Thomas might now seem obliged to argue that all the faithful who are in the course of actually attaining perfection in the Church will have to be chaste, poor and obedient – have to give up the highest created goods: namely, marriage and family, possessions, and personal self-determination. But it would go against the Church's tradition, and indeed against each generation's experience, to say that only those who follow the evangelical counsels – virginity, poverty and obedience to a rule of life interpreted by a superior – can reach the perfection of charity. All Christians are called to such perfection, but not all Christians are called to be Religious.

So Thomas is confronted here with an antinomy: there are two truths, both of which have to be affirmed, albeit on distinct kinds of ground, yet they seem to be mutually exclusive. Thomas solves the problem in typical Scholastic guise, by making a distinction. Perfection can be thought of, says Thomas, is two ways: either, 'essentially', in terms of what it is in itself, or 'instrumentally', in terms of what best or most

---

[6] Ibid., a. 2, corpus.

readily brings perfection about.[7] Applying this distinction, Thomas comes up with the following conclusions. Essentially, perfection consists in charity. Instrumentally, it consists in the life of the counsels which are ordered to charity in a specially helpful way. So for Aquinas it is because the life of the counsels – virginity for the kingdom, poverty for discipleship, and obedience to rule and superior in a common life – is perfection *instrumentaliter* that those who commit their freedom in a binding way to the pursuit of the counsels can be said to be in the 'state of perfection', even though *essentialiter* perfection is not asceticism, nor monasticism, nor the Religious life, but charity. Thomas deals directly with the misunderstanding of the concept of the state of perfection which is sometimes encountered in modern times when he says that 'nothing forbids some from being perfect who are not in the state of perfection, and nothing prevents others from being in the state of perfection who are not perfect.'[8]

The Vows

In that state, vows play for Thomas a notable role. Vows were much more important in Religious life for Thomas and for mediaeval theologians generally than had been the case for the Fathers of the Church.[9] John Cassian and Augustine show no awareness of vows, nor is there any evidence of an act of formal commitment among the desert fathers. Probably, as with the Syrians, monastic life was seen as a carrying out of the baptismal vows, an actualisation of the baptismal covenant. However, there *is* evidence for public professions of

---

[7] Ibid., a. 3.
[8] Ibid., a. 4.
[9] C. Justice, 'Evolution of the Teaching on Commitment by Monastic Vows from New Testament Times to the Ninth Century', *Cistercian Studies* XII (1977), pp. 18–40. See also P. Séjourné, OP, 'Voeu', *Dictionnaire de Théologie catholique* 15.2 (1950), cols. 3182–3234; idem., 'Voeux de religion', ibid., cols. 3234–3281, and C. Capelle, *Le Voeu d'obéissance des origines au XIIe siècle* (Paris, 1959).

virginity in the presence of the Church, and I have been calling public virginity not only 'asceticism' but 'proto-monasticism'. At the start of the fourth century, local synods, one at Ancyra (modern Ankara, the Turkish capital) and one at Elvira in Spain, issued canons dealing with men and women (or in the Spanish case, just women) who had earlier dedicated themselves to God through a public expression of their intention to practise virginity, but subsequently went back on their word.[10] Such promises were explicitly required by Basil,[11] and Augustine refers to a particular nun who had got into trouble as a *professa sanctimonialis*, a 'professed Religious'.

Not the same as a vow yet associated with the idea of a new beginning in the Christian life was the ritual act where, in the sixth-century East, as witnessed by Denys, monks were blessed at the time of receiving the habit.[12] Seemingly, this influenced Western practice somewhat later, especially among the Benedictines, where prayers for such a ceremony were added to the provisions about the acceptance of novices in the Rule of St Benedict.[13]

That is reflected in the Dominican profession ceremony when the habit and its wearer are blessed not, however, when the habit is received but after the taking of first vows (which, until the later nineteenth century, were the only vows).

Historians are divided on the question: Were vows, in the full sense of solemn promises to God, ever made before the early Middle Ages? Certainly some sort of promising was known fairly early on. Were these promises to God or simply promises made in the presence of representatives of the Church? When, in the Rule of St Benedict, the monk promises

---

[10] S. Elm, *Virgins of God. The Making of Asceticism in Late Antiquity* (Oxford, 1994), pp. 25–29.
[11] Basil, *The Longer Rules*,15.
[12] See more widely, P. Raffin, OP, *Les rituels orientaux de la Profession monastique* (Bellefontaine, 1974, 2nd edition).
[13] R. Yeo, *The Structure and Content of Monastic Profession* (Rome, 1982), pp. 266–270, 283–288.

obedience, stability and *conversatio morum*, i.e. renunciation so as to attain full conversion of life, this seems to be a matter of promises made to the abbot and community in God's presence rather than, strictly speaking, promises to God.[14] A similar ambiguity is found in the Celtic monastic sources. Not until the twelfth century, with the canon regular Hugh of St Victor, someone Thomas occasionally cites as among the *moderni* or 'modern doctors', do we get a clear account of the vow in the sense in which the Church has subsequently understood it.

If we ask, why was there this development of giving greater weight to vows actually made directly to God, we simultaneously enter into St Thomas's theology of what a vow is. The most satisfactory answer to the question, why did vows come to take on in the West an importance they had never had previously (and, so far as I am aware, would never in fact gain in the Christian East), has to do with the advent of the Western Christian humanism of the twelfth century. For that humanism, of which the Cistercian writers such as Bernard are the most obvious representatives, freedom is a precondition of love, while the gift of love in freedom engages the whole self. Like other mediaeval writers, Thomas had given more thought than did the Fathers to the fact that Religious life is a way of deploying human freedom. As we saw, for Thomas a 'state' is a particular condition of being situated in life through the exercise of freedom. This leads to Thomas's reason for stressing the importance of the vows.

Religious perfection, argues Thomas, requires us to offer our whole life to God. But we cannot in any ordinary sense give our whole life to God here and now. Our life is not a simultaneous whole. It is lived successively, spread out through future time. So the only way we can give our whole life to God is by the obligation of a vow. Vows enable us to give

---

[14] Benedict, *Rule*, 58.

ourselves totally to God in a form of life whose disciplines, or exercises, find their meaning in three vows in particular: poverty, chastity and obedience. The 'disciplines or exercises' Thomas is thinking of are listed by him, not necessarily exhaustively, as prayer, *lectio* or spiritual readings, keeping vigil, fasting and (more vaguely) 'good works'. These practices, which for him make up the concrete texture of Religious life as a God-ward life, find their own interpretation in the vows. Although the Dominican took only one vow, the vow of obedience, Thomas has no hesitation in identifying three vows as central. The Franciscans were the first to make this explicit in their profession formula, with a great impact on succeeding Religious foundations.

That these particular three vows – poverty, chastity, obedience – are the essential ones is clear, says Thomas, if we bear in mind three key features of Religious life as found in the observances – the 'disciplines or exercises' – which make up its *de facto* structure. The vows make sense of what one does concretely as a Religious if the Religious life is, first, a way of life that tends toward the perfection of charity; secondly, a kind of life that frees the soul from external cares, and, thirdly, a holocaust or total sacrifice whereby one offers oneself to God. In all of these respects, but especially the last, solemn promises of poverty, chastity and obedience make sense. By these three vows we offer to God the good that is external things (poverty), the good that is our own body (chastity) and the good that is our own will, and so the use of all the powers of our soul (obedience). So these three promises serve to integrate the Religious life, itself made up of various practices, into a unitary thing.

In the specific Dominican tradition with its single vow, obedience is understood as a kind of global vow which commits one to all the values of the Dominican way of life – the three evangelical counsels, the common life, preaching (the distinctive apostolic work), and everything contained in the law of the Order, thus regular observance, study, the mode of governance practised and so on. The Dominican profession formula mirrors that used in the Middle Ages by reformed canons, notably the Premonstratensians, but also the canons of Osma of whom St Dominic had been one. It is a typical profession vow of canons which has been extended by replacing the reference to a particular church and substituting for it reference to a universal Order.

The variety of Religious Orders in the West

This reminds us that there is in the Church, especially in the Latin Church, a great variety of Orders and communities. Thomas thinks it important to offer a comment on this, and indeed it has sometimes been criticised, notably by the Eastern Orthodox, as obscuring the unity of the monastic state. For Thomas, while Religious life is indeed one, it can also be differentiated, in two respects. There can be legitimate diversity of observance because one can, for instance, dispose oneself to chastity either by solitude in the eremitical life or by common living in the coenobitical life. And then there is also a legitimate diversity in the end to which different groupings of Religious are directed. Even though contemplation is the primary goal of every Religious, some kinds of active works, useful to the Church, are both expressive of the love of neighbour and also fully compatible with the Religious state.

In his exploration of different sorts of Christian life in the 'Second Part' of the *Summa theologiae*, Thomas argues that to apply oneself to the spiritual welfare of one's neighbour is the greatest service one can do for them – and this Religious do when they use spiritual weapons to defend the faithful against error and temptation. So as to preach and teach efficaciously along these lines, there must be study, and study, says Thomas, so far from detracting from what is proper to the Religious life as such, actually promotes it. Study assists the contemplation of divine things. It also, he suggests, helps in the keeping of the vows. Study helps chastity by turning away the mind from lascivious thoughts and mortifying the flesh through what he describes as its own laboriousness. It also helps poverty by eliminating the desire for wealth as one comes to prefer wisdom to riches. Finally, study helps obedience by deepening our grasp of the Word of God and its commands.

It is obvious that Thomas has the Dominicans especially in mind (as is pointed out in the Introduction to the [Edwardian] English translation.)[15] Yet he does not say so in as many words, and indeed in no writing of his that is universally accepted as genuine does Aquinas so much as mention the name of St Dominic (the disputed case is the *Letter to Brother John on How to Study*). What is perhaps more surprising is that, when on two occasions secular masters in the University of Paris attacked the friars as an illegitimate development of monasticism, Thomas's replies – the little treatises *Contra impugnantes* and *Contra retrahentes* – maintain the same reserve.[16] Evidently, he did not wish to be described as simply defending his own: the institution to which he happened to belong. Instead, he wanted to set out the wider principles which make space for Religious who combine with the essentials of monasticism a life of study that is ordered to teaching and preaching, including the highly individual preaching entailed in hearing the confessions of penitents. Thomas is thinking of Religious who are not parish clergy (that did not really need saying in his day), and hold no pastoral charge in the Church.

One reply might have run: the Religious in question were a variety of canons regular – though this would not have helped the Franciscans, who were also included in the secular masters' indictment. But Thomas knew of canonical tractates which spoke of canons regular as themselves monastics of a kind –

---

[15] Thomas Aquinas, *An Apology for the Religious Orders* (London, 1902).
[16] There is an excellent account of these controversies in J.-P. Torrell, OP, *Initiation à Saint Thomas d'Aquin. Sa personne et son oeuvre* (Fribourg, 1993), pp. 109–139.

and spoke of them so quite properly if we take the long patristic view of these matters, rather than just refer to the Carolingian legislation, which distinguished sharply between *ordo monasticus* and *ordo canonicus*. Cited against the friars was a letter of St Jerome which famously described the task of a monk as to 'mourn': that is, to do penance for his sins and those of others, and precisely not to 'teach'.[17] The patristic sources we have scanned in this book suggest that was hardly an adequate summary of the rich meaning given to the monastic life in the age of the Fathers, but incontrovertibly it was what a high authority, one of the four Latin doctors, had said about the matter. Much of Thomas's reply is concerned with pointing out how little representative this citation was even of Jerome's own writing, for in another letter the great biblical scholar had advised a monk so to live within the monastery that he would be able, as a cleric, to teach others.[18] And what, asks Thomas, of those Fathers who had been simultaneously monks and theologians, such as (his examples) in the East Gregory Nazianzen, Basil and John Chrysostom, or in the West Gregory the Great and Augustine and, indeed, for that matter, Jerome himself who, in the prologue to his Latin translation of the Bible, had promised to give instruction about Holy Scripture? And leaving aside these particular models it just seems to be the case that monastics, by the primarily contemplative bent of their lives, will become more fit, not less fit, to transmit to others what Thomas calls 'heavenly teachings'. There is also a very practical dimension to this in Thomas's mind. As he writes:

> It is ridiculous to assert that a man is rendered incapable of teaching because he has adopted a life which gives him more quiet and greater facility for study and learning.[19]

---

[17] Jerome, *To Riparius and Desiderius, against Vigilantius*.
[18] Idem., *To Rusticus*.
[19] Thomas Aquinas, *Against those who Impugn the Worship of God and Religious Life*, 2.

And even if – granted for the sake of argument but not conceded – it were true to say that monks cannot teach *precisely as monks*, what about monastics who are ordained, whether as bishops, priests, or even deacons? What about, for instance, those canons regular?

Thomas's defending the legitimacy of monastics taking on the role of teachers in the Church is paralleled in what he has to say about Religious who preach and hear confessions. Preaching, so he says in *Contra impugnantes*, is a ministry especially befitting the state of perfection which Religious profess. Professed for such a state of life, Religious can 'the more earnestly instruct their hearers to love heavenly things',[20] and he adds, moving once again from the sublime to the pragmatic, Religious also have the advantage over the parish clergy that they are not diverted from the preparation of their preaching by the demands of ecclesiastical administration or the many different good works to which parish priests must give attention for the sake of the temporal well-being of their flock. And as to confessing penitents, Thomas points to the example of the Eastern Church where, he says, nearly all the confessors are monks. This is an interesting (and rare) example of his reporting, not so much the texts of the Greek fathers which for him is fairly habitual but, rather, what is customarily done in the *practice* of the Greek East: in this case, one might hazard, he was basing himself on his contacts with those who had lived in the Crusader kingdoms where, as we know, he had correspondents. Thomas admits that monastics have no right to preach or hear confession without the mandate of a bishop or, supremely, of the Pope. But, as he points out, the secular clergy also need a canonical mandate of an episcopal kind. It is not enough for them simply to be ordained. They must have a pastoral charge.

Thomas has established in principle, then, that monastics, where suitably qualified, can carry out ecclesial actions such as

---

[20] Ibid., 4.

these. And the welfare of the faithful (also described as 'the common good of the Church') may well be enhanced when apostolic monks minister by teaching, preaching and hearing confessions. That, thinks Thomas, should suffice by itself to move bishops to action.

People object, he reports, by asking: How can monastics live a mortified existence if they are going to be turning themselves into academics and surrogate pastors? Thomas's reply is they will not turn themselves into academics and surrogate pastors if they persist in the 'austerities' that are at once proper to the monastic way and compatible with the life of study which prepares the way for such teaching and preaching. The examples he gives are 'vigils' and 'fasting', though he also adds 'and the like'.[21] Such Religious will give up manual labour, true, but that is only another example of such austerities, done, as with the desert fathers, to keep monks from indolence. Yes, they replace by spiritual exercises the more straightforward physical work the Apostle of the Gentiles, Paul the tent-maker, did. But we are living in the post-apostolic age when preachers can no longer rely, as the apostles could, on the internal inspiration of the Holy Spirit, but must prepare themselves for their task by the equally demanding work of study.

Though Thomas is implicitly defending two Orders in particular that had been created as recently as the twenty years immediately preceding his birth, he does not accept that these new institutes are seriously innovative. Instead he looks to the patristic precedents, as found in the texts to which he had access, and also, as we have seen, to the contemporary practice of the Eastern Church. For him, the Religious life is a single – we might well go so far as to say 'unitary' – state in the Church the representatives of which can and should, however, be drawn upon in such a way that the wider needs of the faithful

---

[21] Ibid., 5.

are met. He would not, I think, have disagreed with those today who say that the chief problem of Religious life in the Western Catholic Church is that its fundamental monastic identity, which should be the source of its distinctive practices, ethos, and spirituality, has been excessively overlaid by other preoccupations.

Conclusion

In this book I have argued, in the first place, that the Religious life is a homogeneous development from the New Testament itself. The monastic way, so far from being specialized and even exotic, is the simplest and most basic form of Christian discipleship.[1] And I have also made the further claim that in its achieved form – at the end of a 'trajectory' starting in the Gospels – it is the product, both as theory and as practice, of the patristic age. There is nothing of substantial importance in the practices that make up the Religious life that post-dates the Church of the Fathers. Likewise, all the chief themes of theological reflection on the significance of the Religious life derive from teaching that is already explicit in this zone or that of the patristic world. The new movements of the early Middle Ages, whether in the monastic order or the canonical order or, indeed, the eremitical order (which by its refusal of *pure* coenobitic living is distinct from both of these), are to be seen as fundamentally movements of *ressourcement*, of going back to the sources – which means to say, in the case under discussion, to the monastic Fathers.

What is new among the great Orders of the high mediaeval epoch – the pastoral outreach of the Premonstratensians, the

---

[1] Fortunately, I am not alone in this view: see for instance the essay by the great Toulouse Thomist Michel-Marie Labourdette, OP, 'Signification de la vie religieuse dans l'Eglise', *Revue thomiste* LXXI (1971), pp. 480–493.

moral preaching of the Franciscans, the doctrinal teaching activity of the Dominicans – is novel only in species, not in genus. These developments mirror the way that, centuries before, the patristic episcopate, many of whom were monk-bishops, sought to use monastics for the prosecution of a variety of legitimate ecclesial objectives, whether in education, nursing, or missionary activity. To take, once again, by way of illustration the example of St Dominic:

> St Dominic rejects nothing of the spiritual tradition of the Church, one and holy, or at any rate nothing of what is compatible with his intuition of an Order at the service of preaching. He has no care for originality, locating himself in the wisdom experience of the fathers of the desert, in the ideal of unanimity of the Rule of St Augustine, in the austerities of Grandmont or the monastic life he knew and appreciated among his Cistercian friends.[2]

I draw a general conclusion, thinking not juridically but theologically. There is no forest of trees called 'the Religious Orders of the Catholic Church'. There is only one tree with many branches. The tree is the monastic estate, the branches are the diverse forms of life the members of that estate can take up, combined with the different missions in the Church to which they can be mandated.

This thesis, if true, has wide-ranging consequences, not least for the later Religious Orders and Congregations, and the most recent 'new movements' of the Catholic Church after the Second Vatican Council, some of which have groups of ascetics at their heart. All need to recover the great lines of monastic spirituality as the common basis of their call in the Church. That is so notwithstanding the specificities of

---

[2] G. Bedouelle, OP, *Saint Dominique, ou la grâce de la Parole* (Paris, 1982), p. 234.

emphasis of this or that founder or the particularities of function they envisaged for their Institute. To put the same point rather differently (and even more provocatively!), the Religious of the Latin Church need to emulate the monks and nuns of Orthodoxy. They need to see themselves as a single body with a shared contemplative spirit. Of course there will be differences between them, just as there are, in fact, in the history of Orthodox monasticism (the Church of Russia has considerable experience of this). But there will also be a unity – and a greater assurance about just where the fonts of inspiration are to be found.

Index

Aaron 46
Adam 46
Ambrose 7, 9, 43
Anthony viii, 8, 9, 10, 13–18, 28, 29, 43, 54
Aphraates 34
Aquinas, see Thomas Aquinas
Athanasius viii, 7, 8, 9, 10, 16, 17
Athenagoras 5
Augustine viii, 4, 7, 24, 26, 38, 40, 42, 43-49, 50, 52, 58, 59, 65, 66, 69, 75, 80

Basil 37-38, 50, 54, 75
Benedict viii, 23, 26, 37, 52–54, 55, 58, 59
Benedict of Aniane 54, 58
Benedict XVI 47
Bernard 60, 66, 71

Camelot, T. 7
Cassiodorus 53
Cassian, see John Cassian
Catherine of Siena 7
Chadwick, H. 44, 48
Chitty, D. 29
Clement, pope 5, 6
Clement of Alexandria 6
Cyprian 6

Decius 14

Denys 67
Diego 56
Dominic 21, 56, 58, 65, 74, 80

Elijah 29
Ephrem 34
Euthymius 31

Farrelly, B. 61

Gregory of the Great 75
Gregory Nazianzen 40-41, 75
Gregory of Nyssa 7

Hilary of Poitiers 8, 43
Hugh of Lacerta 58
Hugh of St Victor 71
Hume, B. vii

Ignatius of Antioch 5
Isaias, Abba 30

Jerome 4, 13, 14, 26, 43, 75
John, evangelist 5, 65
John the Baptist 3, 29
John Cassian viii, 11, 21–24, 28, 30, 42, 54, 60, 65, 69
John Chrysostom 7, 22, 75
John the Hesychast 31
John Paul II 5, 6–7
Jordan of Saxony 60

Josephus 4
Judas Iscariot 10

Koester, H. 1–2

Lausias 28
Luke, evangelist 10
Luther, M. 1

Macarius of Alexandria 17, 26
Martin of Tours, 43
Matthew, evangelist 8
Methodius 6-7

Norbert 60–61

Origen 7, 22

Pachomius 14, 24–27, 43, 50, 54
Palladius 28
Paul, apostle 4, 33, 65, 77
Paul of Thebes 13, 14
Paulinus 9

Peter Damian 57
Philo 4
Plato 6
Plotinus 17, 37
Polycarp 5
Porphyry 17, 37

Robinson, J. 1–2
Rose of Lima 7

Sabas 31
Sebastian 53
Sixtus III 53
Stephen of Muret 57
Stewart, C. 22

Tertullian 6
Thomas Aquinas ix, 5, 11, 60, 63, 64–78

Victor 60

Ware, K. 31

www.ingramcontent.com/pod-product-compliance
Lightning Source LLC
Chambersburg PA
CBHW020016050426
42450CB00005B/505